WITHDRAWN

CHANGEMAKER

CHANGEMAKER
W. Harry Davis

EDITED BY LORI STURDEVANT

Afton Historical Society Press

AFTON, MINNESOTA

*Afton Historical
Society Press*

P.O. Box 100, Afton, MN 55001

800-436-8443

aftonpress@aftonpress.com
www.aftonpress.com

Frontispiece: W. Harry Davis with students at the new W. Harry Davis Academy
© 2003 STAR TRIBUNE/Minneapolis–St. Paul

COPYEDITED BY MICHELE HODGSON
DESIGNED BY MARY SUSAN OLESON
PRINTED BY PETTIT NETWORK, INC., AFTON, MINNESOTA

Library of Congress Cataloging-in-Publication Data
Davis, W. Harry, 1923–
Changemaker / W. Harry Davis; edited by Lori Sturdevant.
   p. cm.
Summary: The autobiography of a man who grew up in the segregated city of Minneapolis, Minnesota, in the early twentieth century and became active in the civil-rights movement of the 1960s.
ISBN 1-890434-60-4 (alk. paper)
1. Davis, W. Harry, 1923—Juvenile literature. 2. African American civil-rights workers—Minnesota—Minneapolis—Biography—Juvenile literature. 3. Civil-rights workers—Minnesota—Minneapolis—Biography—Juvenile literature. 4. African Americans—Civil rights—Minnesota—Minneapolis—History—20th century—Juvenile literature. 5. Minneapolis (Minn.)—Race relations—Juvenile literature. 6. Minneapolis (Minn.)—Biography—Juvenile literature. 7. Boxing trainers—Minnesota—Minneapolis—Biography—Juvenile literature. [1. Davis, W. Harry, 1923– 2. African Americans—Civil rights—Minnesota—Minneapolis. 3. Civil-rights workers. 4. Race relations. 5. Boxing trainers. 6. African Americans—Biography.] I. Sturdevant, Lori, 1953– II. Title.
F614.M553D38 2003
977.6'57905'092—dc21

                                   2003005426

Printed in China

*The Afton Historical Society Press
publishes exceptional books on regional subjects.*

W. Duncan MacMillan
President

Patricia Condon Johnston
Publisher

Contents

A word to teachers

CHANGEMAKER is a book with several possible uses in the classroom. It simply might be read by students, perhaps as a supplement to other material that informs young people about the civil-rights movement of the twentieth century. It might occasion the keeping of a reader's journal, as Harry Davis suggests. Possible questions and suggestions to prompt entries in a reader's journal appear at the end of each chapter. You may want to pick and choose among them or to provide journaling prompts of your own. Several of the suggested journal topics would lend themselves to classroom discussion.

Changemaker might also inspire one or more of the class projects recommended at the end of several chapters. Again, we invite you to be selective in choosing among them. If your class includes children whose older relatives experienced the civil-rights movement, you might want to use those family members as additional resources, perhaps for a class oral-history project.

Harry Davis and I hope that **Changemaker** contributes material useful to you as you seek to teach students one of the most important lessons of history—namely, that it will soon be their task to make history themselves.

Lori Sturdevant

Acknowledgments

WE ARE INDEBTED to the many people who helped us produce **Overcoming,** from which **Changemaker** directly descends. For this volume, particular thanks must go to Patricia Johnston and her staff at Afton Historical Society Press, who saw in our first volume the germ of its offspring. Special thanks also to Harry Davis's cousin Vera F. Carter, who, as the Harper family historian, added and verified many a detail, and to Lori Sturdevant's daughter Emelia Carroll and Harry Davis's granddaughter Chloe Davis. These two sixth-graders advised us on phrasing and content appropriate for their peers. It has been a long time since either of us was in elementary school, so we were glad to have the assistance of two young readers with more recent experience.

L. S. and W. H. D.

Harry Davis with Chloe Davis and Emelia Carroll.

Dear young reader,

THIS BOOK is more than the story of my life. It's also the story of an important part of our country's history—the effort to create equal opportunity for people of all races. That is a story that is not yet finished. It continues to affect every American, even young people like you.

That is why I was pleased when Patricia Johnston at Afton Historical Society Press suggested that I adapt for young readers my autobiography, **Overcoming,** published by Afton Press in 2002. I believe you need to know about things that happened before you were born to understand the world you live in now, and the world you will shape in the future.

I call this version of my autobiography **Changemaker** because I did more than witness change in the lives of black people in Minneapolis. I helped create changes that would make life better for people of color. I also tried to make something positive out of the changes that came my way. I want you to know my story so you can begin to think of yourself as a changemaker too.

Change is a constant force in life. It has already been a big part of your life, and there is a lot more change ahead. Your body will change. Your world will broaden. You will meet people who are different from you. You will encounter things that you think are unfair or harmful or wrong, things that need correcting. You will see that while some changes just happen, other changes are made to happen by people with the courage to dream and the ability to speak and act.

You need to know that as an American, you are free, no matter the color of your skin. You can express your thoughts in ways that affect the thinking of other people. If you learn to use the tools of citizenship guaranteed to us in the U.S. Constitution and the Bill of Rights, you too can bring about change for the better.

Here is one way for you to learn from this book: read it with a notebook or journal handy. At the end of each chapter, you will find questions or suggestions intended to make you think about your own ability to be a changemaker. Write your thoughts in your journal. When you have finished, you'll have your own handbook for understanding and making change.

Some of the chapters also include some ideas for projects that you and your class might do together. You might be able to help your teacher decide which project is right for your class.

I hope that reading my story will give you some ideas about what is possible for you.

W. Harry Davis

Foun1ding

DRIVERS SEE ONLY pavement when they cruise past the junction of Olson Memorial Highway and Interstate 94 in north Minneapolis today. In my mind's eye, I see much more. I knew that spot when it was the wild corner of Sixth and Lyndale Avenues North. It was the one place in otherwise quiet Minneapolis where people could come to gamble, get drunk, and do other outlawed things during the 1920s. Some people called it the Hellhole. I called it home.

The Hellhole was home to Minnesota's largest African American and Jewish populations. They were there because the white majority in Minneapolis would not allow them to buy houses or rent apartments anywhere else in the city. In my neighborhood, gangsters lived side by side with doctors, merchants, laborers, and loving families.

This is the only photo I have of my father, Leland Davis. It was taken late in his life.

I am the child of one of those families, the youngest of six children born to Leland C. and Elizabeth Jackson Davis. Like many people of color who came to Minnesota after slavery ended in America, my parents were the products of hardship, endurance, and courage. My grandparents and great-grandparents were people of several races who had in common a great capacity for love.

My father was known as Leland or Lee Davis as an adult, but that is not the name he was given at birth. I do not know that name. He was Winnebago Sioux Indian, born on that tribe's reservation in Nebraska in July 1887. His mother, whom we called Grandma Molly, was a small woman with straight black hair and flashing eyes. She was a daughter of the tribe's chief, Golden Eagle. I don't know anything about my dad's father. Dad and

U.S. Army sergeant John Wesley Harper, my
great-grandfather.

Molly left him behind when they left the reservation, when Dad was about five years old. They moved east across Nebraska to Omaha. Molly gave Dad the name Leland as she enrolled him in public school.

I never was told why Dad and Molly decided to strike out on their own. It was a brave thing for them to do. The 1890s were bitter years for the Sioux, a time of defeat, loss, hunger, and oppression. Molly may have understood before others in her tribe that the old way of life was gone forever and that she needed to make her way in a different world. She was stubborn and spirited. My mother used to say of her, "If she butted heads with a bull, she'd win."

While Molly was in Omaha, she met a black man with skin nearly the color of hers. His name was Abner Davis. He owned a barbershop in Omaha's black neighborhood. That was quite an accomplishment for a former slave, which he was. We don't know when he was born nor where, other than in the southern United States. We don't know whether he escaped from slavery or was freed at the end of the Civil War. He was part of a westward movement of former slaves after that war, set on making a new life. Many of them settled in Kansas. He swung north and landed in Omaha.

Maybe the fact that they were both refugees from lives they had once known is what brought Molly and Abner together. They married, and my father took the name Davis. Molly and Abner also had a son of their own, Clarence Davis—my Uncle Dixie.

Molly and Abner eventually moved to Minneapolis. Grandma Molly was joined by a relative—likely an uncle—who was called Grandpa Mac by me and nearly everybody else in his last years. He lived to be 109, long enough for me to get to know him well. When I was seven or eight years old, Grandpa Mac used to visit us on summer evenings. He would sit on the porch, Indian-style, with a blanket wrapped around him, and tell the children stories about the Civil War and the buffalo hunts of his childhood. He told of the arrival of large numbers of white and black people on the Great Plains, and how the Indians soon noticed that white people treated black people badly. Whites insisted on staying separate from blacks and would tell the Indian leaders to do the same. "They'll steal your daughters," the white people warned. Those warnings only served to make Indians feel friendly toward blacks.

We kids listened closely because Grandpa Mac

talked just above a whisper. He seemed to have a sixth sense, an ability to predict the future. We children were in awe of him. Though he was very old, Grandpa Mac could always remember the name of every child. For some reason, he started calling me "Little Pops." Soon other members of the family called me "Little Pops" too. The nickname stuck.

Like my father's family, my mother's people were touched deeply by events in American history. My great-grandfather on my mother's side was John Wesley Harper, a white man born in 1839 in Wheeling, a city that was then in Virginia and now in West Virginia. He was the son of a slave-owning family. His father would travel to Norfolk, Virginia, to buy slaves. Young John Wesley may have joined his father on one fateful trip in the 1850s, when the purchases included a young girl who had been forced off her plantation home in Opelousas, Louisiana. Her name was Frances Ann Frazier.

Frances Ann was unwanted property on the plantation where she was raised because she was plainly not the daughter of a black father. Her skin was fair, much lighter than that of other slaves. Her father was likely a member of the plantation owner's family. When she grew up, her owners sold her to a slave trader and forced her to leave her home. She was given the name of her owners, Frazier, as she was shipped off to market. There is no record that she ever saw her family again.

Frances and John may have met as slave and owner,

Frances Frazier Harper, my great-grandmother.

but their relationship developed into something much more positive—though it probably was not seen as a good thing by John's family and friends. We can only assume that the disapproval of the Harper family was behind the young couple's move to Zanesville, Ohio, about the time of the outbreak of the Civil War. Ohio was a haven for escapees from southern slavery. Daring and passion must have been required for these two young people to run away and start life over together. Their daughter (my grandmother) used to say that her father was a little bit crazy. Maybe that helped.

When the war broke out, John enlisted in the Union army, joining the fight to free the slaves. When the war ended, he stayed in uniform. John Wesley Harper became a career sergeant and took his wife and growing family with him to a series of army posts on the nation's frontier. My grandmother, Armintha Alice, was the second of their children to survive infancy; she was born at Fort Bliss,

Texas, on March 8, 1872. Her youngest sister, Evelyn Belle, came twelve babies and eighteen years later, on September 18, 1890, at Fort Snelling, Minnesota. It was the last assignment of John's army career. The Harper family had finally come home.

It was at Fort Snelling that Armintha met and married William Henry Jackson in the early 1890s. I regret not knowing more about my Grandpa Jackson. He was a black soldier, born five years after the end of the Civil War in a place unknown to my generation. As a black man, he wasn't allowed to become an army officer. He made his career in the army as a barber. His life came to an early end at age fifty-two, the year before I was born.

Armintha Harper Jackson, my grandmother (left), and her sister Frances Murray.

He liked to gamble and had taken to playing high-stakes card games on Washington Avenue in Minneapolis, a white man's street. One night, a group followed him out of the gambling parlor and beat him to death.

The Jacksons had fourteen children. My mother, Elizabeth Frances, was the third surviving child and the second daughter. She was born in 1898. Even as a young girl, she was a favorite of my grandmother. Grandma taught my mother to cook in the same southern style she had learned from her Louisiana-born mother. She knew how to fix many different kinds of greens, fried potatoes, and the traditional meat dish from the slave cabins: chitlins. My grandmother could fix chitlins and all types of meat from the pig, including the ears and the feet, with black-eyed peas and greens, and make it taste out of this world. Grandma was also the family medicine woman, and she taught my mother the homemade remedies that Frances Frazier had learned on the plantation. Grandma even taught my mother to brew homemade beer, though my mother was a strict churchwoman and would never drink the stuff she made.

Grandma was the family's master sergeant. The relatives all jumped to attention every time she came into a room. She was smart, strong, and strict. When she told a grandchild to do something, she meant it. She would spank a youngster with a stick if he or she were out of line. But Grandma was loving too. After my grandfather died, it didn't take her long to remarry. Her second husband and the man I knew as Grandpa was Sam Bell, a horse doctor at Fort Snelling. He had been a friend of Grandpa Jackson and was well acquainted with the large family before he joined it.

Everybody, including her own children, called my mother Libby. She spent most of her girlhood in north Minneapolis. But the connection the Harper and Jackson families had with Fort Snelling gave her a somewhat larger world than many of her neighborhood-bound peers. For example, she occasionally went with her father to social events at the old fort or with other male family members to semiprofessional baseball games at old Nicollet Field on the city's predominantly white South Side. It was there, at an exhibition game between the Minneapolis Millers and the Kansas City Monarchs of the Negro League, that she was spotted in the stands behind the Monarchs' dugout by the team's catcher, my father, Leland Davis. Leland was twenty-three; Libby was just twelve. The year was 1910.

By that time, my father had been playing Negro League baseball for at least four years. He started playing ball for money with a famous touring baseball team called the House of Davids. My dad got a tryout with them when they came to Omaha to play an exhibition game at a time when they were short a catcher. He got hired on the spot. Some time later, when the House of Davids played an exhibition game with the Kansas City Monarchs, he got a quick promotion. Along with the Chicago American Giants, the Birmingham Black Barons, the New York Black Yanks, and several others, the Kansas City Monarchs were early mainstays in the Negro League. (The Monarchs became the league's most successful team—but that's years ahead of our story.) The Monarchs were impressed by my dad's play and also by the fact that his bronze skin left people guessing about his race. He did not look out of place on an all-black team.

It was as a Monarch that he met Libby at Nicollet Field. She must have made quite an impression, for what happened that day could have been little more than happy talk between ballplayer and fan. Names and addresses must have been exchanged. Both Leland and Libby resumed their different lives after that first meeting. But something important had happened for both of them.

Later that season, my dad was traded—sold, actually, for the teams treated the players like livestock—to the Chicago American Giants. As he did at the end of every season, he looked for a job. This time, he came to Minneapolis to find work—and to look up pretty little Libby. The job he landed was as a driver, first of a team of horses, later of a truck, for Rose Brothers Lumber and Cleveland Wrecking Company. It was close to my mother's neighborhood. He became the first Native American professional truck driver in Minnesota.

Few men of color in Minneapolis had better jobs in those years. The best jobs open to blacks were on the railroad as a Pullman porter, a waiter, or a chef. Next best was to hold a similar position at one of the big downtown hotels. At some businesses, blacks were hired as doormen or had shoeshine stands in the lobbies of office buildings. Those deemed most trustworthy would stay in the buildings after hours and clean them. None of these would be considered good jobs today, but the African American people with those jobs then were the lucky ones. Many others did not have steady work.

Maybe it was because my father had two impressive positions—truck driver and professional baseball player—that my grandmother and grandfather agreed to let their second-eldest daughter marry him when she was only fourteen and he was eleven years older. Maybe they had come to know my quiet father as the dependable man he was. Maybe they simply became resigned to a romance they could not stop. My parents were married on August 6, 1912.

Dad kept playing professional baseball after he and Libby were married because the money he could make was needed at home. When he was playing, he was able to send home $25 every other week—a comfortable amount of money for those years, even for a family that was growing rapidly.

Four children, three girls and a boy, were born to the Davis family between 1913 and 1917. Charlotte Marie came first, in 1913. We called her Dooney, for reasons I do not know. She was an attractive young lady, with high cheekbones that revealed her Native American heritage and wavy black hair that Grandma Molly loved to braid. She was the big sister we younger children had to mind when our mother was not home.

Two years later came my only brother, Leland Clarence, whom we called Menzy. He was a great athlete and a wonderful brother to me. When I was small, he was like a second father. It was his job to cut wood and bring in coal to keep our stoves going in the winter. He hated that job, but he did it well. He had a strong temper (a family trait), and he was big and strong enough to scare you when he was riled up. But he was kind to me. We shared a bedroom.

Geraldine Francis was born next, in 1916, just a year after Menzy. She was fair-skinned, pretty, soft-spoken, and sensitive. She cared a lot about her looks and about boys. That made her kind of wild as a teenager. With one of my mother's younger sisters, she would sneak down to Sixth Avenue and visit the nightclubs. My aunt made sure that nobody bothered her, but my dad would be furious when he found out where she had been.

My third sister, Marie Melrose, was born the next year. We called her Retie. She was a happy, sweet girl. Sadly, she died when she was ten years old. She was playing on a swing at Sumner Field when some tough older boys, including two brothers, came to the park with a bottle of liquor to drink. One of the brothers pushed her swing too hard, and she fell out of the swing and landed on her head. The blow killed her.

That was a horrible time for our family. We all loved Retie so much. I was only four when it happened, but I remember how awful she looked when they brought her body home from the funeral home. In those years, it was customary to place a casket in the front window of a house and have people walk by on the front porch to pay their respects. That went on for three long days before her funeral at Wayman African Methodist Episcopal Church. Retie's death made our family life sad for a long time.

By then, Dad was retired from professional baseball. It turned out that one of the last Negro League games he played was against his old team, the Kansas City Monarchs. The rookie pitcher that day was Satchel Paige, who went on to be, arguably, the best pitcher of all time.

After he left baseball, Lee Davis was a full-time truck driver. He drove a truck for a chain of specialty grocery stores and restaurants owned by two Greek families with ties to our neighborhood. When I was small, Dad would sometimes take me along on his route. It was a big thrill to ride in his truck.

Dad still played baseball on the side, for fun and for pocket money. He got to know black ballplayers in Minneapolis and St. Paul, talented players who were barred from the white teams in town, and recruited them for a new team called the Twin Cities Colored Giants. That team became an attraction with Dad as its coach. He was good at working with young players. When the Kansas City Monarchs came to play an exhibition game, they were

Elizabeth Jackson Davis, my mother, circa 1941.

so impressed with my dad's teams that they would immediately hire some of his players.

My brother, Menzy, joined them when he was thirteen or fourteen. Dad encouraged it, partly to help Menzy deal with his anger and grief after Retie's death. Menzy was about six feet tall, and even as a kid he weighed nearly two hundred pounds. My dad had taught him to be a pitcher, and he was a good one. And, man, could he hit a baseball! At one exhibition game in the old Nicollet Ballpark, at the corner of Nicollet Avenue and Lake Street, he hit a ball that crossed Nicollet and crashed through the awning on a store window and broke the window. The awnings were supposed to protect the windows as the balls would bounce off of them, but they weren't strong enough to withstand Menzy's slam. Only a handful of other players ever broke those windows.

I was always so proud to watch Dad and Menzy play. Even when he was past his prime, my dad could do what great catchers bragged about: he could throw a ball quickly and accurately to second base without leaving the catcher's crouched position. He was not a tall man—he was about my height, five-foot-seven—but he was strong. He used to roll fifty-five gallon barrels of peanut oil in and out of his truck, and lift and throw big, bulging sacks of peanuts. Dad had such ability that he surely would have been a star in Major League Baseball, if only he had been allowed to play. The big leagues would not accept black players until 1947.

Teams in the white Southern Minnesota League—Shakopee, New Ulm, Sleepy Eye, Mankato—used to hire my dad and some of the other Colored Giants to play a few games for them. The money was good—$150 for one game. He put benches in the back of his truck so he could drive his players to Shakopee and installed shades on the open sides of the truck so the players could change into their baseball uniforms when they arrived. They were not allowed to change with the white players.

I was along one fall day in Shakopee when Dad and one of his teammates were playing for the Shakopee team in a championship with the team from Prior Lake. They won the game for Shakopee. I watched as all the other players joined the fans afterward for a big party with plenty of food and drink. Dad and his friend did not go along; they stayed on the diamond. Eventually, someone brought them a plate of food and they stayed on the diamond to eat. I asked Dad, "Why don't we just go with everybody else? You just played for them and everybody

cheered for you." He said, "You don't understand." Dad and his friend were not welcome to eat with the rest of the team, even though they had just won the game for them. It was the same in other towns, I later learned. When they traveled farther from home and had to stay overnight, no hotel in those Minnesota towns would accept them. They had to sleep in Dad's truck. Dad had come to accept such injustice as a fact of life. I was not so accepting. I thought about what I had witnessed that day for a long time.

My mother worked hard, raising a large family and taking care of her younger brothers and sisters. She was a strong woman. She was also a loving person who brought out the best in the people around her. She could make friends just walking down the street. When she'd smile, you couldn't help but smile back.

A fifth baby came into our family in 1920, my sister Eva Juanita. Some years later, my parents also took into their home our cousin Joyce Pettiford. She was the youngest child of my mother's older sister, Frances, who had nine children and died giving birth to Joyce. By then, my mother had six children of her own. She had four other sisters who might have raised Frances's baby. But my mother had always been the responsible big sister in the Jackson family. Joyce was raised as a sister to us.

That was the family I joined when I was born April 12, 1923. I was named for my mother's eldest brother, William Harry.

In your Changemaker journal:

Describe your own family's journey.
Where were your parents born?
Where did they live as children? Where did they meet?
Where were you born?
Where have you lived?
Tell what you know about the reasons for your family's moves.
Did moving make life better for the people in your family?

Or

Ask an adult to describe a decision that made a big
change in his or her life.
Ask how the decision was made, how it felt at the time
to make the decision, and whether it appears now to have
been a good decision. Record what he or she says.

Little Pops

I WAS A NORMAL, active toddler until one day shortly after my second birthday. A contagious disease called infantile paralysis—later known as polio—swept through the Twin Cities. Hundreds, perhaps thousands, of children were stricken. I was one of them. My mother had been reading about the disease in the newspaper, so she

Me, at age fifteen months. Photographers went door to door in Minneapolis in the 1920s, offering parents photos of their children in goat carts. I was stricken with polio less than a year later.

responded with alarm when I started complaining about numbness and pain in my legs. She took me to Minneapolis General Hospital (now Hennepin County Medical Center), where the doctors told her I had the dreaded illness. It was poorly understood, and they didn't know how to treat me.

Meanwhile, I had become paralyzed. My legs could not move from the hips down. I had been a little guy who loved to run, and all of a sudden I could not. I was frightened, and the ache in my legs was severe enough to make me cry.

Libby was the family medicine woman, and her medicine was as good as anything the doctors could prescribe. From years of treating my dad's sports injuries, and from the passed-down knowledge of how to treat the sore muscles of field slaves, she knew that heat and massage could work wonders on disabled limbs. That is what she tried on me. She would fill a tub with water and heat it on the stove until it was piping hot, but not hot enough to burn me, and then she would put me in the tub and massage my legs. Then she would blend wintergreen, goose grease, and alcohol and rub that on my legs from my hips to my toes. She repeated this treatment three or four times a day. At bedtime, after the same process, Libby wrapped my legs in hot bath towels. Then she took a hot iron and pressed it on the towels for what seemed a long time so there would be a steady application of heat to my legs. She was doing the right things.

Life gradually came back into my legs. My left leg responded first and more fully. Before long, I could hop around on my left leg. My right leg remained rather numb. I could feel the hot packs on that leg, but I could not feel a pinprick. After about a year, some feeling returned to the right leg, but the feeling was pain. My right foot was stiff and curling up toward my shin because the tendons in my foot were shrinking. When I cried in complaint, Libby would make some kind of syrup. Using the name Grandpa Mac gave me, she would ask, "Little Pops, does your leg hurt?" If I said yes, then she would give me a teaspoon of the stuff she had brewed. I never knew what it contained. It eased the pain and loosened the muscles, but it could not cure the problem.

When I was five and it was time for me to start school, I could hop on my left leg and hobble around a little on the heel of my right foot, but I could not walk normally. I was deemed a crippled child, and as such I was assigned to the one public school in Minneapolis devoted to the education of handicapped children: Michael Dowling School. It was far from my neighborhood. Every child at that school had a physical disability, often involving their arms or legs. In 1928, I was the only child of color in the entire school. Several nurses worked at the school every day, and some were teachers too. A special bus—navy blue with a white stripe—picked up Dowling children at their homes. My brother, Menzy, used to carry me and place me safely on the bus in the mornings. After school, either Menzy or one of my uncles would be there to carry me off again. In addition to the driver, a female bus attendant trained to deal with medical emergencies rode the bus. She was nice to the kids.

I was examined when I first got to Michael Dowling and was told I should use a brace on my right leg. It was a metal brace with a special shoe built into it. When I put the brace on, I stepped my foot right in the shoe and tied it up. In the heel there was a metal part with rubber on the bottom, which allowed me to walk on my heel more easily. The brace was uncomfortable at first, but it helped me use my right leg. It made me one of the more mobile students in my class. At first, I thought that was why I was always left behind on Tuesdays and Thursdays, when groups of children would go to the nearby Shriners Hospital for heat and massage therapy on their ailing limbs. Later I learned the real reason I did not go to Shriners: in those years, black children were not welcome to be treated there.

I felt less left out after school when I was back in my neighborhood and able to play at Sumner Field, the park near our home. I was a bit of a curiosity to the other kids because of my brace and limp, but I joined in the play all the same.

I was in second or third grade when my teacher announced the arrival of someone who would change my life. "We're going to have a visitor here for quite a while," she said. "His name is Dr. Paul Giessler." Paul William Giessler was an orthopedic surgeon, a doctor who specialized in the treatment of bone problems. Though he was born in Minneapolis in 1885, he spoke with a thick German accent. He was both a professor at the University of Minnesota and the head of orthopedics at Minneapolis General Hospital. He was famous for developing a surgical technique that could restore movement to disabled limbs. It was said to work especially well with children, whose bodies were still developing.

I met Dr. Giessler a few days later when the principal brought him into each classroom. He was something of a fascination to us. His German accent made him hard to understand, but I was drawn to this gentle man with his nice smile. He flashed that big smile when he examined me. His touch was so tender that I could tell he had love in his heart.

Some days later, the principal came to our room and spoke to my teacher, who then read the names of six classmates whom Dr. Giessler believed he could help. All of them were children with paralyzed legs and arms. My name was on the list. I went home that day wondering, "Gee, what is he going to do with me?"

I soon found out. Dr. Giessler reappeared on a Tuesday, when the rest of my class was at therapy at Shriners Hospital and I was left behind. He was walking by my room when he noticed me sitting alone. He came in and asked me, in his thick accent, "Heddy, vat are you doing? You're supposed to be at the Shriners Hospital?" I said, "I don't know, Dr. Giessler. They don't take me." He smiled and put a big hand on my head. "You and I are going to have a good time," he said. "Starting next week, ve are going to ride downtown in a car, and you and I are going to be together."

That sounded fine to me. The next Tuesday, as he promised, Dr. Giessler came for me. Outside the school, a fancy old Packard car drove up. It had been furnished for our use by a local charity. I felt special to be able to ride in a car like that with Dr. Giessler. The other Dowling kids were impressed.

It was the first of a number of weekly trips I made with Dr. Giessler from school to Minneapolis General Hospital. He made them fun. During our rides, he said, "Heddy, I vant you to be my teacher." I'd say, "OK, if I can, Dr. Giessler." He said, "Vhen I mispronounce a vord that you know, I vant you to tell me vhat the vord is." So I tried to help him conquer his accent. I would say, "Instead of 'vell,' say, 'You're getting *well*,' like *well* water." Then he would laugh and laugh. Our driver would join in the merriment. Any nervousness I had about going to the hospital flew away in the laughter.

Dr. Giessler told me that he would do for me what the doctors at Shriners Hospital were doing for my classmates. He had a device that looked like a metal shield, covered on the inside with light bulbs. He put me on a table, covered my leg with a towel, then placed this shield on my leg. He said, "I'm going to pull this switch and all the lights are going to go on, and you'll feel the heat on your legs. That's what they do at Shriners Hospital." I recognized how similar it was to what my mother had done for me since I was two.

One day he took me into an examining room, put me on a table, and held my foot. He felt where the tendon on the top of my foot was tight. He studied it for a while, then took an indelible pencil and drew a line on the top of my foot. It was where he would make an incision. I was to have surgery. He did that examination for about three successive weeks, not always drawing the line in the same place, as if he were uncertain how to proceed. On one of our drives from school he advised me, "Today, I'm going to have some other doctors come in, and they are going to draw some pictures on your foot too. It won't hurt you; it will just tickle."

Then he started to explain to me: "Inside your foot there is a tendon, like a muscle, that moves your foot back and forth, like you do your other one. What has happened

is that the tendon in your right foot is shrinking. It's attached to the front part of your foot, so your foot is curling back. I'm going to open that up and cut the tendon and add some catgut to the two sides and stitch them back together so your foot will drop down. After that heals, we're going to give you some exercise to make you move your foot back and forth. You tell your mother that when we do this, you won't go to school for a while. When we schedule the surgery, I'm going to pick you up at your house in one of these cars, and we're going to go directly to General Hospital. Tell your mother we want her to go with us."

So that was the plan. He asked me to fill my mother in because we did not have a telephone, and he could not quickly inform her himself. But it seemed that my mother always knew what Dr. Giessler was doing. Perhaps there had been an exchange of letters or a visit at our house that I did not know about. I felt proud one day at the hospital when I overheard Dr. Giessler say to another doctor, "Look what his mother did to the left leg and look what she's done to the right leg. You can move it. Just think of the knowledge she had—to understand that there was soreness in the legs and it had to be treated." I am convinced that my mother saved my left leg. Her medicine had just one limitation: Nothing she did could lengthen that shrinking tendon. Only surgery could do that.

On the big day, I was scared. So many strangers were fussing over me. But Dr. Giessler was wonderful in explaining every detail of the surgery to me and to my mother.

He said, "Harry, we're going to take you into this little room on the side. We're going to put a gown on you and a thing on your head. Then we're going to take you into a room, and I'll wheel you underneath a bunch of lights. There are going to be nurses and doctors all around. What I'm going to do is cut open your foot. When I reach these tendons, I'm going to cut them and attach this catgut to each end, so that your foot will drop down. We're going to hold that so you can't move it until it heals. When it heals, we're going to see if you can move your foot back and forth. . . . We're going to put something over your face." That was ether, a gas that would knock me out. "Then you will go to sleep. When you wake up, we'll be all through with all of this."

The procedure lasted five or six hours. It was a long and fretful day for my mother. She stayed in the waiting room the whole time; my dad joined her after he got off work. He drove his truck downtown because we did not have a car and parked it right in front of the hospital. By the time he got there, I was out of surgery. All I could see, when I came to, was a cast from my hip down to my toes. It kept my leg straight and perfectly still. I was awake when Dr. Giessler came to tell my parents about the surgery. He used a pen to draw a little diagram on the cast. Then he signed his name to it. That signature was something to brag about when I got back to school.

My cast was on for six weeks and nearly drove me nuts. My leg itched terribly, and I could not scratch it. The cast was awfully heavy. I used crutches with it and got pretty good with them. I could spin around on one crutch. I was a happy boy when Dr. Giessler announced, "Tomorrow, Harry, we're going to take the cast off." He did that procedure right at Michael Dowling School and arranged for my mother to be present. He took us into a room where he used scary-looking scissorslike things to cut the cast all the way down the side of my right leg. When he pulled it open, he saw that my leg had shrunk. It was smaller than my left leg. I started to move my foot up and down. Dr. Giessler watched for a moment, then declared, "Your right leg is going to be shorter and smaller than the other, but you're going to be able to walk!" I looked at my mother and she was crying. Dr. Giessler was so happy, he was shouting. I was too. What a moment that was!

I walked on crutches for another month. Almost every day, Dr. Giessler would come to Dowling School and check on me. After a few days, he would take the crutches away and ask me to walk short distances. I still was not allowed to go to Shriners Hospital for therapy, so Dr. Giessler became my therapist as well as my doctor. He would not let me go without the care I needed just because of prejudice. He gave me wonderful encouragement as I learned again how to walk and run.

I was walking steadily and running a little within six weeks, and running pretty well within three months. I hadn't run since I was two years old, so I had no clear memory of what it was like. You forget even the most basic skills if you don't practice them. My mother would take me to Phyllis Wheatley Settlement House after school to give me more practice running at a place where an instructor could watch me. I was sometimes discouraged, but then those kind instructors would say, "Let's have a hopping contest." They knew that I could outhop any kid who was used to having two good legs.

Before the end of fourth grade, Dr. Giessler had a talk with my teacher and principal at Michael Dowling School. "Harry is doing well enough now that he won't have to stay here," he told them. "He can go to his neighborhood school now." They didn't wait until the end of the year to move me; I was told I would start at Sumner School the following Monday. My teacher cried as she said good-bye to me that Friday afternoon. She said over and over, "I'm going to miss you here. I'm going to miss you." The principal came in to say good-bye too. Then in came Dr. Giessler. He hugged me and said, "I don't want you to forget me. I won't forget you."

With that, I was off to Sumner School and a more typical life as a north-Minneapolis kid in the 1930s. And with that, Dr. Giessler, the man who saved me from being handicapped, left my life, only to reappear many years later. It was 1946, and I was trying to piece together a living after having been laid off from a defense-plant job. With another man in a similar fix, I went into the home-maintenance business. Our specialty was removing storm windows in the spring and replacing them in the fall.

One day when we were working at a big house near Lake Harriet, I noticed I was being watched by a man in a wheelchair inside the house. As I moved from window to window, he moved too, watching me. I smiled and waved at him and he returned the gesture. Finally, he motioned for me to raise the window, which I did. He said, "Young man, I cannot help thinking that I know you. What is your name?" When I told him, his jaw dropped, then he burst into a big grin. "Harry, I'm Dr. Giessler!" he said. I did not recognize him. He had aged beyond his years and was himself now unable to walk. Heart disease had shortened his career. We renewed our friendship that day, and I stayed in touch with him for the rest of his life. He lived only a few more years.

Polio left me with a right leg that would always be shorter and weaker than the left. But the physical damage didn't bother me much. I could not be a runner, but I could high-jump well. I could play quarterback in football, pitch a mean softball, and play for short periods on the basketball court. The more significant impact of polio may have been on my personality. I had learned early in life how to endure pain, how to get along with others from a position of weakness, and how to find happiness when things are not perfect. I saw the worst thing that had ever happened to me overcome through the knowledge and kindness of another human being. Polio made me believe in the power of kindness.

In your Changemaker journal:

Write about a time when illness or injury struck you or someone you know. What did it take to recover?
If full recovery did not come, what changes had to be made to adjust to continuing illness or disability?

A project for your class:

Learn about infantile paralysis, or polio. Divide into research teams and assign each team to find out about some aspect of the disease. Some things to find out: What causes polio? How did it spread? Who were the following people and organizations and what did they do to help people with polio: Elizabeth Kenny, Franklin Roosevelt, Jonas Salk, the March of Dimes? What is an epidemic? When did some of the biggest epidemics of polio happen? What is paralysis? How was paralysis caused by polio treated? What is vaccination and how does it work? What does eradication mean, and is eradication of polio a possibility?

In the 3 *'hood*

MY MOVE TO SUMNER SCHOOL in fourth grade shrank my world to the neighborhood that some people called the Hellhole. It was a place unlike any other in Minneapolis—more diverse, more dangerous, more disadvantaged, but also, somehow, more alive.

My neighborhood's center was the junction of Sixth and Lyndale Avenues North. Sixth Avenue, or just "the Avenue" for short, was full of shops. Lyndale, which was also Highway 65, was an entertainment street lined with restaurants, bars, and nightclubs. Even during the 1920s and early 1930s, when the sale of alcohol was illegal in the United States, Lyndale was the place to go to get a strong drink. Parlors that were supposed to sell only nonalcoholic near beer would quietly offer their customers a shot of booze called a mickey. Buy a bottle of near beer, pour some in a glass with a mickey, and you have a drink much stronger than regular beer. Kids often saw people staggering as they left near-beer parlors.

Sixth and Lyndale probably had more illegal activity per square foot than any place west of the city of Chicago. But during daytime hours, more of what happened there was legal than illegal. Some storefronts had a split personality. For instance, a tailor shop would also sell policy, an illegal numbers game. Or a drugstore would sell real medicine, but also have illegal drugs available for their "trusted customers." One of the night spots was Howard's Steak House, a restaurant that featured live music—plus activities in the back room that kids weren't supposed to know about. It was owned by Howard Walker, a black fellow from the neighborhood who was a tap dancer and a drummer. Mostly his restaurant served people from other parts of town who came to the Avenue for a night of fun. Those of us who lived there couldn't afford a steak dinner at a restaurant. But Howard let his neighbors know that, for a birthday or special occasion, they could come in early in the evening and he would serve them at a reasonable price.

At Sixth and Dupont, there was a smoke shop

where the big-shot racketeers played high-stakes poker games. It was a dangerous zone. Next door was the Liberty, our neighborhood movie theater. Kids used to go there on Saturday afternoons to see cowboy movies and adventure serials. One afternoon, when I was about ten, some friends and I came out of the theater and saw gangsters standing in front of the smoke shop. A car came careening down the street at high speed, and a submachine gun was poked out a car window. We heard the sound of repeating shots. Several of the guys on the street were hit; one was killed. We saw the blood jump right out of him as he fell over in the gutter. If we had come out a little sooner, we would have been in the line of fire.

That wasn't the only murder I witnessed. We would sometimes see men in fistfights on the street, and then, suddenly, one of them would drop. Someone had pulled a knife or a gun to settle the dispute. One kid I knew watched as his father tried to break up a fight and was shot as a result. That kind of thing was unusual during daylight hours, but at night the activity on the streets was different. When the sun went down, you would hear the mothers calling kids into their homes. The lights would be lit on the Avenue, the music would start, and the mothers would want their children home.

There were a lot of big families in the neighborhood, people with six or seven kids. You would not be acquainted with just one member of the family; you would know them all, and their mothers would know you. The moms of those families had permission from your mother to spank you if you got out of line while you were in their yard or by their house. There were clear standards of discipline, and they were enforced.

Similarly, a store was not just a store to us but a place owned by someone we knew, from a family we knew, who often lived close by. A lot of storekeepers lived in apartments above their stores. Kids knew the good guys and the bad guys in the 'hood. One way we could tell them apart was by the cars they drove. The legitimate people drove Fords, Chevys, and Plymouths, if they owned cars at all. The crooks drove expensive models, like Cords, Auburns, and Packards.

The houses on the streets that ran north and south from Sixth Avenue were typically two-story wooden structures built between 1870 and 1900. They were long, narrow houses, each with a porch in front. They had living and dining rooms, kitchens with cooking stoves that burned wood or gas, small yards, bedrooms upstairs, dirt floors in the cellars. They were well-made houses, but by the 1930s they were showing their age. Few of them had furnaces. The old stoves that provided heat in the winter also guaranteed a cold start to every morning six months of the year. Most houses had indoor plumbing, but when the weather turned cold the pipes would freeze. Then someone had go to the cellar with a newspaper, roll it up, light it like a torch, and run it along the frozen pipes to thaw the ice. All of the houses had electrical power, though it was sometimes cut off when a family failed to pay its utility bill.

In the middle of it all, just a block from Sixth and Lyndale, stood Sumner School. It was a large building, taking up half of a full city block and serving kindergarten through ninth grade. Sumner's principal and teachers saw themselves in a day-to-day battle over the hearts and minds of the neighborhood's kids. The Avenue offered one way of life to children; Sumner School offered another, and was prepared to use some force to keep them from straying. We weren't permitted to leave the school grounds during recess and lunch hour in those years. If any student did, he or she could and would be spanked. Parents gave their permission for spankings. After a child turned ten years old, a parent could give permission for him or her to be spanked by the principal with a belt. Not many kids got that treatment, but we all knew the consequences for misbehavior.

Sumner's student population reflected the neighborhood fairly well. A third to a half of the kids were African Americans. Finns, Scandinavians, and Mexicans mixed with Jewish and black kids. We got along well. There were few fights along racial lines. Sumner School created a feeling of togetherness among the children and convinced us not to worry about each other's color.

The teachers were white, but that did not bother me. They were wonderful. They showed us the same kind of love and discipline we had at home. They would correct students, usually in a nice way like this: "Really, Harry, what good was the fight? I see you've got some bruises. They hurt, don't they? Well, if you don't get into a fight, you don't get bruises." If you had seriously misbehaved, they would say the dreaded words, "I'm going to talk to your mother." Teachers and parents had close relationships in those years, even though not many families had telephones. When a teacher wanted to speak to a parent, she would call the Phyllis Wheatley Settlement House and ask the staff there to relay the message to someone from the family. A message from a teacher was treated with utmost seriousness.

When I started at Sumner School, I was the new kid, even though I was sitting beside children I had seen at Sumner Field for years. I was different. I was small for my age, and my right leg was noticeably shorter and weaker than my left. My hair was wavier than the other black kids' hair. My mother fussed over me and made sure my hair was brushed just so. She would wash my face until she had almost sandpapered it. Those first days, she dressed me in a nice white shirt and neat blue pants, fancier than the other kids wore. My brother said, "Lib, don't dress him like that. Those kids are going to beat him up." My mom replied, "That's my baby! He's got to look nice when he goes to school."

Menzy was right, of course. The other kids teased me, and worse. My mom eventually got the message and stopped her grooming routine, but the teasing and taunting and occasional fistfights continued. Walking home from school became a misery for me.

I was in fifth grade when I came home one spring afternoon to a surprise. My dad's younger half-brother, Clarence, whom we called Dixie, had arrived for a visit. He was a professional boxer, and a good one. He had contended twice for the world middleweight championship. He was in his mid-thirties then, maybe a little past his prime but still an active boxer. His visits with us always came after important matches. He would come to rest and heal his wounds, and begin to train again for the next fight. I had come bruised and limping into the house that day, but I quickly forgot my own wounds when I took a look at Uncle Dixie. He was in much worse shape than I. Still, I must not have looked too good.

"Little Pops, what's the matter?" he asked. I told him about the trouble I was having with school-yard bullies. "I still can't run too fast. I can't get away from them," I said. "Little Pops, you don't need to learn how to run faster," he said. "You need to learn how to box."

I was an eager pupil and my uncle was a good teacher. That very day, we began daily lessons in the art of self-defense. I quickly learned that the thugs that bothered me after school were merely fighters; all they did was throw punches. I was being trained to be a boxer, and that was far better. Boxing begins with the basic punches and stances, but then teaches leverage and balance. It teaches what position to be in to throw punches fast and hard. A boxer learns to bob and weave, to dodge punches and counterpunches.

Uncle Dixie would hold up his hands and I would practice my punches on them, with him telling me what to do. I learned all the basics. There's the straight punch, the one that you throw straight ahead. There's the cross-punch, thrown from right to left or left to right. There's the hook, where you get out and around and strike your opponent on the side of the face. There's the uppercut, which lands underneath an opponent's chin. There's the looper, where you kind of throw your right hand and loop it over and down so it lands on the top part of the opponent's face. I learned what position I had to be in to throw each of the punches. I learned the counterpunch variations on the basic punches so I could deflect punches thrown my way. Fighters simply throw any old punch without thinking. A boxer is always thinking, to make sure his legs and arms move and work together so he is always in control.

I was not just learning what to do, but why. Rope-skipping is an example. People think skipping rope is for building endurance, and it does. But the main reason a boxer skips rope is to build the muscles in the lower calves, ankles, feet, and toes. A boxer needs strong feet and toes. He needs to be quick and surefooted.

Uncle Dixie's stay in Minneapolis was a long one that year, and my lessons ran well into summer vacation. I discovered that as I learned to be a boxer, I was also becoming a better batter in baseball. I was concentrating on my stance and the leverage that comes with a proper swing. I could throw a ball farther and stronger because I thought about how to set my foot for maximum leverage. I applied the same ideas to football and learned how to fake a defender out of position. That summer transformed me from a crippled child into an athlete.

Part of the fun was the closeness I developed with Uncle Dixie. He was single and had no children of his own, but he seemed to have a natural gift for teaching and relating to the young. He spent a great deal of time with me, patiently giving advice, praising me when I did well, hugging me to show how much he cared. He was training for his next fight, and he involved me in that. Sometimes I ran with him when he did his roadwork. We would talk about how to move our legs and feet and how to breathe. When he would compliment me on being a fast learner, that would make me run all the harder and faster. Uncle Dixie was not just teaching; he was giving me the ability and the desire to learn. That made a big difference.

Finally, the day came when Uncle Dixie announced, "The time is up." Both of his wounded eyes had healed. He had an appointment for a fight in another city. As for me, school was about to start. I was soon going to have to face the bullies there. Two boys in particular had been my tormenters. I concocted a plan for dealing with them if they had not dropped their interest in picking on me.

Sure enough, those two were on my tail after school the very first day. I put my plan into action. I still couldn't

Sumner School, on Olson Memorial Highway between Aldrich and Bryant Avenues North. It was built in 1876 and last used as a school in the 1940s.

My ninth-grade graduating class from Sumner School, January 1939. Our teacher was Lilah Sullivan; I am in the second row beside her.

run as fast as those bigger boys, but I could do pretty well for a short distance. I decided to run down Bassett Place, a short, alleylike street. I waited until I knew they were following me, then took off down Bassett Place. One building along that short street housed the Knitting Works, an underwear factory. That building had a large red-brick chimney in back and a narrow passageway just big enough for one person to come through. I led them there because Uncle Dixie told me not to try to fight two people at once. Try to get into a situation that permits facing your opponents one at a time, he had said. That passageway was just the place. I ran and positioned myself between the building and the chimney. They ran after me, one at a time, exactly as I had planned. Then punches flew—and boy, did the punches Uncle Dixie taught me work wonders! That day, finally, I was not the one to come home bloodied and crying.

When I got home, my mother was waiting. "How come you're late?" she asked. "I was kind of fooling around," I said, which didn't fool Libby. "Tell me the truth now. How come you're late?" So I told her what had happened. Even though she knew what grief those boys had caused me, she was less than pleased that I had evened the score. She said, "Mr. Everson [the principal] will probably be calling me because their parents will say that you started it and you beat them up."

Libby was right. The next day, my teacher, Miss Hill, said, "Harry, Mr. Everson wants to see you." She asked the boys I had fought to join me in the principal's office. Then, as I passed by her on the way out the door, she whispered to me, "Nice going, Harry." She had heard what had happened and knew what I had been through the year before. Mr. Everson seemed to know too. He lectured the three of us about not fighting and warned us that our parents would be called if any further incidents occurred. But he did not suggest that I started the trouble.

I didn't have any more trouble with bullies. As word got around school that I had whupped those two toughies, everybody left me alone. I felt as if I was finally welcome in my own neighborhood.

In your Changemaker journal:

Write about an experience you or someone you know has
had with bullies. How was the situation handled?
What lessons did you learn from the experience?
What would you do differently if something similar happens again?

Or

Comment on the way Harry Davis handled the bullies that were
tormenting him.
Do you think he was right to use boxing to defend himself?
Did he have other options?
What would you have done in his situation?

Phyllis 4 Wheatley

THERE WAS ONE PLACE in my neighborhood where I always felt welcome. It was Phyllis Wheatley Settlement House, my second home. The Wheatley was always part of my life, or very nearly so, since it was founded on October 17, 1924, when I was eighteen months old. A settlement house is a place often dedicated to helping immigrants adjust to American life. The Wheatley served a different kind of immigrant—descendents of Africans who had come to the New World in chains as slaves. It was named after Phyllis Wheatley, an eighteenth-century slave girl who had the good fortune to be raised as the foster daughter of a white Boston family and given an education. Wheatley wrote poetry that was known and praised by George Washington.

It's fair to say that Phyllis Wheatley Settlement House is what brought the African Americans of north Minneapolis together into a functioning community. Black people were living in the neighborhood well before the Wheatley was founded, but they weren't living *together*.

The Wheatley provided them with self-awareness and pride. It fostered relationships. It taught people to help one another and to raise their families in a difficult and challenging environment.

The Wheatley's founders were a group of well-to-do white ladies called the Women's Christian Association. They had in mind a place that would help black girls avoid becoming prostitutes. But the vision of the Wheatley's first director and head resident, Gertrude Brown, was much bigger. She wanted the Wheatley to provide black people with services they could not easily get anywhere else in Minneapolis. For example, black students enrolled at the University of Minnesota were not allowed to live in its dormitories, so they were housed at Phyllis Wheatley. Likewise, black entertainers who came to Minneapolis in the 1930s were welcome to perform downtown, but not to stay in downtown hotels. They too stayed at Phyllis Wheatley. Kids coming to the Wheatley after school might bump into Count Basie's or Duke Ellington's famous jazz orchestras, jamming in a vacant classroom to get ready for a show that night.

The Wheatley got its start in a two-story wooden building previously occupied by the Hebrew Talmud Farah School. That building was too small to house Gertrude Brown's vision. In 1929, a large three-level brick structure was built to take its place. It consumed half a city block and was designed to Miss Brown's specifications. It had a big kitchen, dormitory rooms, a gymnasium with a balcony for spectators, a library, classrooms, and space for a nursery school and a clothing distribution center. The building also included an apartment, where Miss Brown lived. She was never off duty.

Miss Brown was a tall, strong woman who never married. Born in Ohio, she was educated at Columbia University in New York and came to Minneapolis when she was thirty-five years old. She was smart and opinionated. Her principal opinion was that black Americans are first-class citizens, deserving the same rights and bearing the same responsibilities as white Americans. Some people called her a troublemaker, for she did not hold back her views; she left no doubt about who was in charge at Phyllis Wheatley. But she was as kind as she was forceful, and she was especially gentle to the children who were Wheatley regulars, like me.

Miss Brown positioned the Wheatley on the front line of the battle for the hearts and minds of the neighborhood's children. After school, boys and girls who did not go straight home had only two choices: They could wander down to the Avenue and see what was happening with the gangsters there. Or they could go to Phyllis Wheatley, where the boys might join a pickup basketball game and the girls might have a cooking or grooming class. No other after-school programs were available for school-age children in those years. Our neighborhood had a park, but its only organized activities were sponsored by Phyllis Wheatley. For example, college students who stayed at Phyllis Wheatley taught neighborhood kids to play tennis on Sumner Field's tennis courts. The only youth sports competition we had was that arranged with other settlement houses by Miss Brown and her staff. The programs were fun. My friends and I chose the Wheatley over the Avenue most days.

Phyllis Wheatley Settlement House, 809 Aldrich Avenue North.

Miss Brown was persuasive; some would call her bossy. At the beginning of every school year, she would get all the neighborhood kids and their parents to come to a meeting in the Wheatley's gymnasium. She would announce the program for the year, telling, not asking, you to participate. "Here's what we're going to have for your children this fall and this winter," she would say, in a long speech that no one dared to interrupt. "You'll have medical examinations here for your children required by the school system. We're going to have organized sports groups. If you're looking at improving your cooking, we have classes for you. We want your teenage girls to attend the cooking classes. We want your teenage sons to come too." Problems at school? The Wheatley can help. Feeling sick? A doctor will be here on Saturdays, seeing people at no charge. Toothache? The dental clinic is in two weeks. A handicapped child? We've got connections to help you. Guys on the Avenue bothering your daughter? Tell Miss Brown. She'll see that it stops.

In my young eyes, Miss Brown was the very definition of leadership. It seemed that she had a hand in everything good that happened in my neighborhood. She was not a civil-rights leader in the sense that the people who came a generation later were. But she was preparing us to take our rightful place in society when that opportunity came. She made sure every child who came to Phyllis Wheatley got the message that he or she was just as good as anyone else.

To her we brought our questions after we experienced an episode of discrimination. Those episodes have a way of staying with a person. I remember going downtown with my mother when I was still quite young. It was a hot day, and we sat on a bench downtown for a long time, waiting for the streetcar to take us home. I wanted to go into one of the lunch counters to eat and to drink something cold, but my mother said no, we couldn't do that. We weren't permitted there, because of the color of our skin. If we wanted to go to a movie theater downtown, we had to sit in the blacks-only balcony. Nearby was the Marigold Ballroom, a dance hall that brought big-name bands to town. African Americans were not welcome there until long after I was grown. But we did not care. We had a dance hall almost as big in our gym at Phyllis Wheatley. In the summer, we had dances outdoors with great bands, food, and soft drinks. The best local black bands played for us because Miss Brown gave them free rehearsal space.

Miss Brown helped shape our attitudes about white people in a way that kept us from becoming racists. When we would come to her with a story about discrimination, she had a ready response: "That was terrible, and the people who did that are bad people. But not all white people are like that. You see our board—they are good people. They care about you. These are the people that built this building so you could come and learn." If we said something disparaging about downtown businessmen, she reminded us, "Those companies contribute money to Phyllis Wheatley every year."

I had an especially close relationship with Miss Brown. I think she felt that I was a special child because of my handicap. When she saw me come in to Phyllis Wheatley, she would hug me and ask me how I was doing. Her extra attention became all the more important to me after a dark day in 1935, when I came home to find my dad loading boxes of his clothes into his truck. I went upstairs and found my mother crying. I said, "Libby, what's the matter?" She said, "Your father just left. He moved out." "Why did he move out?" "We haven't been getting along too well lately. I'm sure you've heard us arguing after you went to bed." I had, but I had not thought much about it. Strong tempers were common in our family.

The breakup of my parents' marriage left me angry, confused, and sad. I felt caught in the middle. I admired my dad. He was so strong, and though he didn't play with us a lot, we knew he loved us. He worked hard to support us. I loved my mother very much. She had raised us kids, often with little help, it seemed.

Much later, I understood better what had happened to them. I saw that my dad was quiet and withdrawn, and not home as much as he should have been. They were very different in ages and interests. Dad was not much of a companion for Libby. Money was always tight, which strains a relationship. I did not understand all of this at the time. When my parents' breakup was a fresh wound,

Gertrude Brown, founding director of Phyllis Wheatley, with some of the neighborhood children. My three sisters, Charlotte, Geraldine, and Marie, are in the group.

I was a mixed-up kid.

Of course, Miss Brown knew what had happened at the Davis house. She had a way of knowing everything in our neighborhood. She was especially kind to me in the weeks after it happened. I think she knew that, as the youngest child in the family, I was more affected by the change than my siblings. She said to me, more than once, "If you need anything, or if you need to talk to somebody, come and see me." Sometimes, I would ask her questions. Her answers eased the pain, but did not cure it.

My own living arrangements changed soon afterward. At first, the Davis house was Libby's house. Then she moved out, Dad moved back in with another woman, and my mother moved into an apartment on Sixth Avenue. I no longer felt comfortable in either place. My oldest sister, Dooney, by then married and the mother of two small children, came to my rescue. I went to live with her, just a few blocks away, with the continued financial support of my father. At Dooney's house, I had my own bedroom. I had a good relationship with my sister. I had responsibilities, like bringing coal from the shed to the stove that provided central heat. But I also had fun, as I took the role of big brother and playmate to Dooney's children.

Dooney's kindness helped me through several rough years. I suffered a fresh blow in 1937, when Gertrude Brown left Phyllis Wheatley. I never knew whether she left voluntarily or if she was pressured to leave by some of the powerful people in Minneapolis who were not prepared in the 1930s to deal with a smart, outspoken black woman. She moved to Washington, D.C., where twelve years later she would be killed in a car accident. Her departure made me feel lost, uncertain, and abandoned.

But she left behind a new head of boys' programs at Phyllis Wheatley who would play a big role in my life. His name was Raymond Hatcher. He came to Minneapolis from Ohio as an expert on teen organizations. He was a no-nonsense, extremely organized person, but he had such a warm personality that even when he was scolding you, you would not get angry with him. He was about thirty years old when he and his wife, Mae, came to Minneapolis shortly before Miss Brown left. They had no children. Mae became head of the girls' department at Phyllis Wheatley.

Ray Hatcher's idea was that every boy at Phyllis Wheatley older than nursery-school age should belong to a club, a group of anywhere from ten to forty boys close to his own age. Ray's clubs were not casual affairs; they were well organized. Ray taught us how to operate them, then coached us afterward about how to improve. The clubs elected officers and learned the responsibilities of a president, vice president, secretary, and treasurer. They learned Robert's Rules of Order, the formal system for operating meetings, and used those rules in their meetings. They paid dues, usually a nickel a meeting. They kept minutes. They decided what activities to pursue. They did work projects around Phyllis Wheatley, earning points that they could redeem for special activities or privileges. The clubs taught us a great deal about how to function in organizations. My club took the nickname of the popular black heavyweight boxing champion, Joe Louis. We were the Brown Bombers.

Ray's timing could hardly have been better for me. Something happened during the summer of 1937, when I was fourteen, that more than ever made me need the structure Ray was creating.

I was one of several kids who liked to get together on hot days and walk west on Sixth Avenue all the way to Theodore Wirth Park, called Glenwood then. The lake beckoned to us in those days when air-conditioning was scarce. Yet we knew that when we went that far west, we were venturing into the territory of a bunch of tough kids who believed in protecting their turf. We knew we had to be prepared to either run or fight. Some of my friends made a point of having me with them. If a fight developed, they wanted me along. I was sort of feeling like a tough guy that year. If someone wanted to see me throw a punch, I was glad to oblige him.

One day toward the end of summer, it happened. About six of us got into a fight with about the same number of kids. One of the kids I punched was knocked unconscious. He was out cold, lying on the ground. His friends got scared and ran home to tell their parents what had happened. Naturally, the parents called the police. Meanwhile, my friends and I retreated to Phyllis Wheatley.

That's where we were when the cops came with some of the boys we fought. They identified me as the one who had thrown the knockout punch. The cops did not believe them at first. "It can't be—he's the smallest one of the bunch!" they said. The boy I knocked out was much larger. We all were ordered to appear in juvenile court.

I was scared to death. It was the first time I had any kind of trouble with the law. I told my mother, and she was willing to go with me downtown to the courthouse. So, bless him, was Ray Hatcher.

The judge asked us what happened. We explained, "Judge, each little area has a gang, and as you go out to Glenwood, you'd better be prepared to fight or you'd better be prepared to run. That day, we decided we weren't going to run. They were going to stop us from going to the lake, so we got into a fight." He said, "Which one of you fought this kid right here?" I raised my hand. The judge looked first at the kid I fought, then at me, and said, "It can't be." He was assured that I had administered the knockout blow. Then he uttered a threat that I later learned was a scare tactic. He said, "What we're going to have to do is, we're going to have to send some of you to Glen Lake"—a juvenile corrections facility. I was terrified of being sent to that place. I knew of kids who had been sent to Glen Lake and who wound up a few years later in juvenile reform schools in Red Wing or St. Cloud, or in the state prison in Stillwater.

But then the judge mentioned the alternative he

really favored: probation, under the supervision of a probation officer. Ray Hatcher spoke up. He said, "Judge, I'm the boys' director at Phyllis Wheatley." He explained his new club system and that I would be part of a club. "I'm going to teach them not to fight in the street. The *Minneapolis Star* has started a boys boxing program called the Golden Gloves. We've signed up with the *Star* to have a team. If you're going to put them on probation, let me be their probation officer." The judge agreed. I was to be

on probation for six months. Ray was to report to the judge on my behavior. Ray even invited the judge to come to Phyllis Wheatley and watch the Brown Bombers box. The judge said he just might do that. "I especially want to see what that little guy is doing," the judge said, meaning me. "If he can already handle the big guys like that, he must be pretty good." I left that courtroom very curious about what Ray had said. I couldn't wait to find out more about the Golden Gloves.

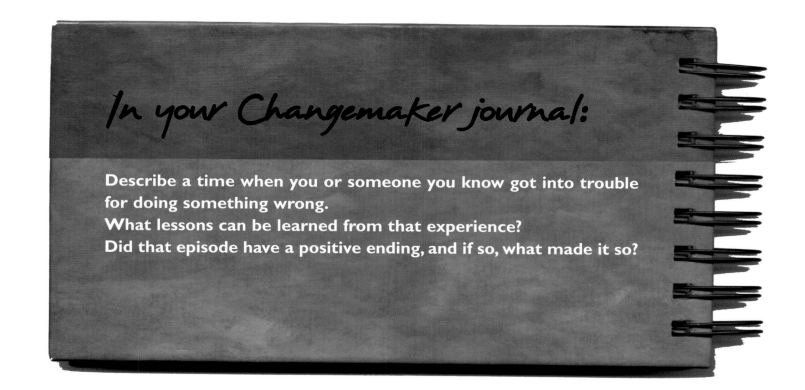

In your Changemaker journal:

Describe a time when you or someone you know got into trouble for doing something wrong.
What lessons can be learned from that experience?
Did that episode have a positive ending, and if so, what made it so?

Preparing 5

THE GOLDEN GLOVES amateur boxing program was started by the *Chicago Tribune* and the *New York Daily News* in the late 1920s. It took off in Minneapolis when the *Minneapolis Star* adopted the program in 1935. The newspaper thought that boxing was good for boys and for the community, not to mention good for newspaper sales and advertising. The *Star*—which eventually merged with the *Minneapolis Journal* and the *Minneapolis Tribune* to become the *Star Tribune*—set up competing Golden Gloves units in community centers in Minneapolis and throughout the Upper Midwest.

It's hard to appreciate today how popular boxing was in America in the 1930s. There were fewer professional sports teams then. Boxing fans considered it an activity that rewarded ability and hard work, and nothing more. That was not always true at the professional level. Crooked fight promoters sometimes controlled the outcome so they could make money gambling on the matches. But at the amateur level, boxing was a clean and honorable sport in which any healthy boy of any size could compete.

Ray Hatcher was happy to say yes when the *Minneapolis Star* proposed establishing a Golden Gloves program at Phyllis Wheatley. Whenever he would catch a couple of boys fighting, he would make them come to the gym, put on gloves, and box, not fight. He insisted on clean fights, with no dirty punches. He had help from a heavyweight professional boxer named Webster Epperson, who had persuaded Miss Brown to let him stay at Phyllis Wheatley while he was in town training for his next fight. Miss Brown had made her standard arrangement: "If you're going to stay here, you're going to have to provide something." Web did the coaching and Ray did the organizing. They made a good combination. In my case, Web picked up where my Uncle Dixie left off in my training. When he first asked me to throw some punches, he said, "You're going to be a good boxer some of these days." But after he got a good look at my right leg, he said, "I don't know. Maybe you won't be able to go those long rounds." But Ray always said I could do it. "Just watch him," he would say.

I made believers of the spectators at Phyllis Wheatley. The first year, I won the right to represent our settlement house in the city Golden Gloves tournament in the featherweight class. I weighed 126 pounds and had been seriously training as a boxer for only a few months. I was starting to think that my leg would not hold me back. But the city tournament showed me otherwise. At that time, the tournament sometimes required a boxer to fight twice in one evening. By the second of two matches, my right leg began failing me. I won a few matches in the city tournament, but I did not impress any observers.

The next spring, I entered North High School as a tenth-grader. In those years, there were eleven high schools in Minneapolis, each serving grades ten through twelve. Classes were staggered, with some beginning their academic year in the fall semester and some in the spring. I was in the spring-semester class in 1939.

North was the largest high school in Minnesota in those years. Today, it is racially well integrated, but it was less so in 1939. Perhaps 10 percent of North High students were African American. Like other city schools then, it had a boxing team. Golden Gloves encouraged its boxers to be part of their school teams. I made the North team, and between Golden Gloves and school I fell into a disciplined training routine. My skills improved. North's athletic director, Tom Kennedy, would say, "You box the way I'd like to have all my kids box." As a result of my experience at the first Golden Gloves tournament, I knew what losing felt like, and I did not like it. I resolved that, as a tenth-grader, I would be a winner.

That year, I represented North High in the city high-school boxing tournament and won in my weight class. It was the first time I had scored a personal triumph in an athletic competition. If I was not already hooked on boxing, winning that tournament set the hook for good. The following year, I won the tournament again, this time in the 135-pound weight division. I was what was known as an aggressive counterpuncher. It's the style of a boxer and a fighter combined. A counterpuncher studies the boxing style of the other fellow and knows when and where he's going to punch. Then he beats the other fellow to the

My schoolmate Matt Hammond (right) and I posed after receiving our North High letters for boxing in 1939. Matt was one of seven brothers; I coached many of them at Phyllis Wheatley.

punch. He has to be quick and strategic in his moves. That's just what Uncle Dixie taught me in fifth grade.

At North, I was also enjoying success in the classroom. My grades were good, especially from my junior year forward. I qualified for a new club called the Pinnacle Society, a sort of honor society for African Americans led by a teacher I admired named Miss Quelo. She was one of the few teachers at North who participated in activities at Phyllis Wheatley. Her goal was to raise our sights so we could see larger possibilities for our futures. She talked often about being prepared to go to college. "Don't think that because others recommend that you not go to college, you should give up on that dream. You're as bright as anyone." I became the first president of the Pinnacle Society, and Miss Quelo seemed to take a special interest in me. She had a brand-new 1940 blue Plymouth and would sometimes say to me, "Harry, why don't you drive my Plymouth up to the garage and get gas and get it washed?" That was a favor I gladly performed.

I was a good student, but not a perfect one. I was known to skip school now and then, especially when the weather turned warm in the spring. That's when Wirth Lake—the one called Glenwood until it was renamed in 1939—would beckon. Some of us would meet before school on Plymouth Avenue and Fremont. One person would say, "Boy, I'd like to sit down at Glenwood today." Then another one would say it, and the first thing you knew, you had six or seven kids going down Plymouth Avenue toward Glenwood. The trick then would be to forge a note of excuse from our mothers to give to the school's attendance clerk the next day so we could claim an excused absence for playing hooky. Having a girlfriend with handwriting like a mother's was a great help.

I also continued with the Golden Gloves program during those years. Several members of my Brown Bombers Club boxed with me. I competed in Golden Gloves at the city level but never advanced to the regional tournament. My leg held me back. But I was able to play other sports recreationally with the Bombers—basketball, football, and baseball. Ray Hatcher saw each activity as an opportunity to teach us how to organize. We kids made a budget for every activity, helped arrange the competition schedule, and decided how to raise money to pay for it. We competed with other settlement houses around the city. Ray helped us select our coach from among Wheatley volunteers and college students. For example, we chose Horace Bell, a University of Minnesota placekicker who was staying at Phyllis Wheatley, as our football coach. He was as strong as a bull. We would hold a ball for him at Sumner Field near Bryant Avenue, and he would kick it two blocks, to Dupont.

The Bombers became good friends, but the relationship that meant the most to me was with Ray Hatcher. He was more of a teacher than a coach, and what he was teaching me, more than anything, was how to teach. I came to admire his interest in the structure of any activity, including boxing. He taught me that winning was a matter not of luck, but of work. You study for it. You train for it. And whatever you gain, Ray always said, you're obliged to pass along to someone else, someone younger.

Ray was not just teaching boxing. He was always weaving in lessons for life. He had a message that came to mean a great deal to me: "Pay attention to three things, your body, your mind, and your spirit. If you treat them right, they'll treat you right. Don't misuse or abuse them. If you do, they won't be there when you need them." He would hammer away: "Your mind should be full of knowledge. The only way you can get it is by reading and listening and seeing. Listen to the people who have knowledge. Watch what they do and try to imitate them. . . . Your body needs to be physically developed to keep up with your mind. If you're feeling sick, it creates a problem with your brain. Keep your body in good shape." He would stress regular exercise and tell us to participate in sports. He always added: "None of these things is any good if you don't have a relationship with God. You won't love yourself or anyone else if you don't know that God loves you."

One of Ray's lessons involved bus trips to Stillwater State Prison or the Boys' Reformatory in St. Cloud. He would arrange for our Golden Gloves team to put on a boxing exhibition for the inmates. He also arranged for us to have a tour. He wanted us to stay just long enough to sense the stifling feeling of prison confinement and to see some of the faces we recognized from our neighborhood.

Ray would say, "Remember that smart guy? There he is. If you want to be like him, you can be right here." He wanted us to see the consequences of the life some people on the Avenue were leading.

The Avenue did not hold the attraction for me that it had for some other kids. I was busy at school and at Phyllis Wheatley. Besides, I didn't care for what I saw and heard on the Avenue. I knew some of the pimps—the prostitutes' bosses—and I didn't think too much of them. They used foul language of the sort I never heard at Phyllis Wheatley. They called women disrespectful names. After being around Ray Hatcher and Gertrude Brown, I knew better. I could always hear Ray's voice in my head, saying, "Mind, body, spirit." I did drink a little home-brewed liquor once, and, boy, did I get sick! I said to myself, "What fool would want to drink this stuff and get sick every day? Something has to be wrong with that person." Cigarettes? I'd see guys smoking who would cough and cough. "What fool would smoke these cigarettes?" I thought.

About the only thing that appealed to me on the Avenue was the chance to see a big-name musician who might show up at one of the night spots. They wouldn't let teenagers into those places after 10:00 p.m. But if the people at the door knew you and knew that somebody special was there, they might let you in to listen to music or get an autograph.

One day Ray Hatcher announced, "We're going to have a camp." Somehow he learned about available state property southwest of the city, between Shakopee and Savage, along the Minnesota River. It was a former military camp. Instead of cabins, it had barracks, about six of them, each able to house about twenty kids and furnished with double bunk beds. The camp also included a huge dining hall, a kitchen, a well with a pump for plumbing, a big recreation room, and baseball diamonds and playing fields. It had everything one would want for a summer camp, except campers. Sometime during the winter of 1939–1940, Ray persuaded the Phyllis Wheatley board to enter into a ninety-nine-year lease with the state for use of that property as a youth camp.

When spring came, a bunch of us teenagers went to work to turn that deserted campground into Phyllis Wheatley Camp. We cleared the roadway and the grounds, cleaned and painted the buildings, and repaired whatever needed fixing. Meanwhile, Ray and Mae Hatcher were planning an ambitious summer schedule: a week of younger girls, a week of younger boys, a week of older girls, a week of older boys, and so on. The Bombers (by then sixteen- to eighteen-year-olds) and another youth club, the Olympians, were to run the place. We would be camp counselors and maintenance workers.

Since I had taken bookkeeping at North High School, I was to be the bookkeeper for the camp's canteen. It sold candy, cookies, and pop to the campers. I was to keep track of the inventory and the canteen revenues, and work out a system of credit for some of the canteen's

customers. "We've got some kids who can't pay," Ray explained. "So we've given them jobs. I want you to keep a record of the jobs they do. When they come to the canteen, they get paid with a bottle of pop, a candy bar, or whatever." My duties extended to the supervision of some of the work assigned to the campers in exchange for canteen privileges. We raised chickens at the camp, for example, with the idea that at the end of the summer, we

Ray Hatcher, boys' program director at Phyllis Wheatley and my mentor.

would serve the campers and their parents a chicken dinner. One of the canteen jobs involved feeding and tending those chickens. I made sure that job was done right.

It was a good system. It gave me a chance to get better acquainted with a lot of the campers. There was one female camper that I particularly wanted to know better: Charlotte NaPue. Ray caught wind of my feelings. One day he said, "See that little Charlotte NaPue sitting over there by the cabins? Why don't you go over there and sit down and talk with her?" I tried to pretend I was not interested. "We're not supposed to be fraternizing with the campers," I said. But Ray was persistent. He said, "I'll give you permission to do that. I'm going to have Mae [his wife] sit there and watch you." With such encouragement, I could hardly refuse. I got to know Charlotte that summer.

By the end of my junior year, Ray let me know that he wanted me to take a new role in the Golden Gloves. He wanted me to be an assistant coach. It was an offer I could not refuse. I recognized that, because of my handicap, I would always face serious limitations as a boxer. But I thought I could do well as a teacher. I wanted to be like Ray. So when I was a senior at North High School, I didn't box in the high-school tournament. I spent most of my time at Phyllis Wheatley working with the ten- to fifteen-year-olds in the program we called the Junior Golden Gloves. I worked with the boys and wrote reports of my work that went to Ray, and then on up to the Wheatley head resident.

A big part of what attracted me to coaching at Phyllis Wheatley was the chance to work alongside Ray. He had taught me a great deal about how to teach, but I still had a lot to learn, and I wanted to learn it from him. That was not to be. During my senior year, Ray and Mae Hatcher resigned to take a better-paying job in Detroit. That was a real blow. I felt some of the same disappointment and confusion I had known when my parents separated and when Miss Brown left. But I stayed with the path

Ray had set me on, and I discovered that I enjoyed coaching. (Years later, Ray and Mae moved back to Minneapolis. They said they wanted to retire near "their kids," meaning me and my contemporaries at Phyllis Wheatley.)

I also was enjoying the chance to develop another talent at North High and the Wheatley: singing. I came to North High in 1939 with strong vocal-music training at Sumner School. I became one of two African American kids in the North choir and held my chair all three years. Choir gave me a great opportunity to make friends with kids from outside my neighborhood.

One of the reasons I showed promise as a singer was the music training I was getting at Phyllis Wheatley at the same time. Jeanette Dorsey taught drama there as well as music and was a tremendous pianist. She organized those of us who liked to sing into a choir that was called the Southern-aires at first, then later the Wheatley-aires. We learned to sing gospel music, light operas, and operettas. This was a serious vocal-music program. It included a big public performance each spring.

Music had such appeal for me in those years that I was willing to engage in a little illegal behavior to hear a good concert. Along with a bunch of friends, I'd sneak into the Orpheum Theatre when big bands would perform. Admission might be as little as twenty-five cents, but money was dear to all of us then. One of us would come up with a quarter, buy a ticket, and go in. Then he would go to the lobby and help himself to a bunch of the ticket stubs that guests would often drop in the sand-filled ashtrays. Then he would sneak over to the exit doors on the Orpheum's west side, the darker side, where the rest of us would be waiting to come in. If an usher questioned us, we could say, "Here are our ticket stubs!" and look legitimate. We'd run down and take orchestra seats. That was how we heard the jazz greats Duke Ellington, Cab Calloway, and Ella Fitzgerald.

At Phyllis Wheatley, Miss Dorsey liked to organize vocal quartets. I was part of one of them, called the Four Notes. We used to sit on the stairs that led up to the students' quarters and sing a cappella, imitating big-name vocal groups like the Ink Spots and the Mills Brothers until we convinced ourselves that we sounded as good as the real thing. Miss Dorsey took an interest in what we were doing and coached us a bit. Before long, she had us performing at Wheatley programs. One night, she told us she wanted the Four Notes to sing for the Wheatley board. With some nervousness, we went into the meeting room and did our imitation of the Ink Spots. Then we switched tunes and imitated the Mills Brothers. Oh, my, did we get applause!

One of the board members was Mim Himmelman, whose husband was the manager of Brown's Clothing Store. After the board meeting, she asked us, "How would you like to do a radio commercial for Brown's Clothing? You could use one of the songs you just sang." We eagerly accepted and were soon at the recording studios of WDGY Radio. Mrs. Himmelman was there too, just as proud and protective as any agent or talent scout might be.

Then she told us about another opportunity: "You know, the Ink Spots are coming to the Orpheum Theatre in a couple of weeks. They're going to have a contest to see who can best imitate them. The award for the winner is a two weeks' engagement at Curly's," a night spot in downtown Minneapolis. We entered that contest, and sure enough, we won. But that presented a problem. We were all in high school and we weren't supposed to be in a place where liquor was sold. Miss Dorsey played the piano for us when we won the contest, but she refused to accompany us at Curly's. She wanted no part of any place that sold liquor. But we wanted to keep that engagement. We needed the money. So we all grew mustaches and convinced ourselves that they made us look much older than seventeen and eighteen years. We also convinced a friend to replace Miss Dorsey at the piano. We kept quiet about our ages—and we sang at Curly's for two full weeks.

It seemed in the summer of 1941 that our quartet could go far. After Curly's we landed a gig at the Flame, an operation with a bar in Minneapolis and a bar in St. Paul. We spent one week in each place. Then a place called the Happy Hour gave us a two-week engagement. But just when we were beginning to think singing might be a career for us, world events intervened. Draft notices arrived for several of the guys. The Four Notes had a short career after all.

During my sophomore year, I also had a short career as a civil-rights activist. The famous contralto opera singer Marian Anderson came to Minneapolis that February to perform. It was just a few weeks before she made history as the central figure in a nasty discrimination incident in Washington, D.C. She was denied use of a performance hall owned by the Daughters of the American Revolution because she was black. First Lady Eleanor Roosevelt resigned from the DAR in protest, then arranged for Miss Anderson to sing at the Lincoln Memorial instead. Her Easter Sunday open-air concert in 1939 was a huge celebration of liberty and justice for all.

The events in Minneapolis in February foreshadowed that episode. Miss Anderson had been in Minneapolis before and had stayed at Phyllis Wheatley. But this time, she asked for a room at the Dyckman Hotel, one of the city's finest. Her request was denied. The Women's Christian Association publicly protested the hotel's decision. I heard about it with a few friends at Phyllis Wheatley the afternoon the story broke. With us were Wheatley staff members Leo Bohanan and John Thomas, who said, "You guys are teenagers now. We've taught you about civil rights. We want you to go with us to picket the Dyckman Hotel." We could not say no to them, nor to Marian Anderson. Some of us had come to know her a little when she stayed at the Wheatley during earlier visits to the city. She always spoke to us kindly. She was a wonderful lady whom we all admired.

The next day, we were downtown carrying picket signs. It was the first time I had done such a thing, and it felt good. We walked alongside adult members of the local chapter of the National Association for the Advancement of Colored People, as well as several white people who supported our cause. The adults took care to position us young people in such a way that they could shield us should trouble erupt. A little did. We attracted a crowd that taunted us, spit at us, and threw a few things at us. It was my first encounter with ugly racism, and it was frightening.

A few days later, we got word that the Women's Christian Association had negotiated with the Dyckman Hotel and that Marian Anderson would be able to stay there. At first, the Dyckman asked that she enter the hotel in back and ride the freight elevator to her room. But Miss Anderson's negotiators would have none of that. Then the great Dyckman Hotel backed down and made Marian Anderson a guest, the same as any other. Of course, that meant that the other hotels in town would soon admit black guests. We were proud we had played a role in making that change. We had our first inkling that, if we applied the right sort of pressure, we could change the way our city treated its black citizens. A seed had been planted.

In your Changemaker journal:

What skill or interest do you have now that you would be willing to develop through regular practice and training?

Describe what you are already doing to perfect your talent or pursue your interest, and say what more you would be willing to do to become more proficient.

What changes are you willing to make to pursue excellence?

A project for your class:

Divide into research teams and find out what you can about the following people, organizations, and institutions. Report back to your class.

    Golden Gloves of America

    Marian Anderson

    Phyllis Wheatley Community Center

    Phyllis Wheatley

    Duke Ellington

    Minnesota State Prison at Stillwater

Charlotte 6

CHARLOTTE JEAN NAPUE came into the world on August 20, 1926, and into my life fourteen years later. She has been there ever since.

Charlotte was born in Topeka, Kansas, the second oldest child of John and Omagina NaPue. John and Omagina had six children, and John struggled to support that large family, first as a cook for the Soo Line Railroad, then as a car salesman, and later as a laborer for the Works Progress Administration, which was part of President Franklin Roosevelt's "New Deal" economic program. In 1930, when Charlotte was four, the family moved to Minneapolis.

I had little chance to know Charlotte when we were children. I attended Sumner School; she went to Grant. By the time she arrived at Sumner for junior high, I had moved on to North High. Her family went to Border Methodist Church; my mother and I

Charlotte NaPue at about age fourteen, when I met her.

went to Wayman Methodist, and, later, my sister and I attended Zion Baptist. I spent most of my free time at Phyllis Wheatley. Charlotte didn't come to Phyllis Wheatley as often as I did. She was needed at home to help with her younger brothers and sister.

But it was Phyllis Wheatley that eventually got us together—at camp, during the summer of 1940. I was seventeen. Charlotte was just fourteen, but she was a sober, steady fourteen. Her mother had died suddenly two years earlier, and Charlotte had assumed the role of the responsible big sister. Her youngest brother was only three or four when their mother died. Going to camp gave her a rare break from housework. It would be a stretch to say that we had a summer romance at camp, but we did take an interest in each other.

The romance started the next year, when Charlotte began to come to the Friday Night Socials at Phyllis Wheatley. The socials were dances that cost a nickel for admission. They were intended to give kids someplace other than Sixth Avenue to go to have fun. Families felt good about sending their kids to Phyllis Wheatley because they knew the staff would keep an eye on them. I had a lot of female friends. But during the fall and winter of 1940–1941, I started looking for just one girl at the Friday Night Socials, and I got the sense that she came looking for me too.

Charlotte was not like the other girls I knew, who were silly and aggressive with boys. She was "one of the good girls." That was important to me. She behaved like a lady. She was attractive and well groomed, choosing clothes that looked nice but not fancy. She waited to be asked to dance. When some fellows asked her to dance, she would say no. When I asked her, she said yes. She was a very good dancer. We would jitterbug in our own style. There was also a dance called the jelly-roll blues, a slow dance to the blues when couples would do what they called the belly rub. During that dance, Ray Hatcher used to come around and put his hand between couples, saying, "No closer than this." He never needed to interrupt Charlotte and me; she wouldn't let me get that close. She had firm ideas about how to conduct herself. If conversation turned to wild behavior, she would announce, "I don't do those things." Usually, as the dance ended, word would

spread about a party somewhere. Sometimes those were loud, wild parties where drinks flowed. I'll admit that I sometimes went to those after-dance parties. But I never saw Charlotte at one.

I asked others about her and learned about her family from the pastor at Border Church, the Reverend Damon Young. He was a lot like Ray—intelligent, outgoing, and interested in the young people in the community. He told me about Omagina NaPue's death and about Charlotte's sense of duty to her family. I heard how strict John NaPue was and how he depended on his daughter for help at home.

That information also provided the basis for a bond between us. Like Charlotte, I had been forced to grow up quickly. I was still seeing

Charlotte NaPue (left) and Lela Taylor at the Phyllis Wheatley operetta, spring 1941. Charlotte, age fifteen, is wearing her first formal gown.

My North High School graduation picture.

both of my parents in those years, but ours was no longer a regular parent-child relationship. My dad lived with a younger lady, around whom I felt uncomfortable. Libby was living on the Avenue with a boyfriend and with my sister Eva. Though my parents were still part of my life, I felt that in some ways they had left not just each other, but me.

Charlotte and I were schoolmates at North High for just one semester, during the fall of 1941. She was a sophomore and I was a last-term senior, due to graduate in January 1942. By then, we were getting serious in our feelings for each other. I had lost all interest in other girls, and she refused offers of dates from other boys. Most of our dates were at Phyllis Wheatley or elsewhere in the neighborhood. When I wanted to take Charlotte on a real date, say, to a movie downtown, I had to ask her father's permission.

Charlotte was a movie buff and had a standing date with a girlfriend from Border Methodist, Bonnestelle Jones, to take in the early matinee at the Aster Theater downtown on Sundays after church. But on Sunday, December 7, 1941, Bonnestelle couldn't go. She was hospitalized for the removal of her appendix. I happily filled in for her and was sitting beside Charlotte at the Aster before the film began when the theater's manager stepped onto the stage. He announced that earlier that day, the Japanese had attacked the U.S. fleet at Pearl Harbor, Hawaii. I looked at Charlotte with a chill. She did not fully understand what we had heard, but I did and I explained: it meant war.

Our world suddenly changed. I graduated from North High School in January as planned. I had been thinking about finding some way to go to college the following fall, setting sights on the University of Minnesota. Now, those plans had to be set aside. I fully expected to be in the army by fall. A number of my friends were already in uniform.

Relationships suddenly got serious. Couples who had seemed to be only dating were quickly getting married. Guys who were going into the service wanted to make sure their girls would still be there for them when they got home. They did not want to miss out on any part of life. People's attitude about marriage was different in the 1940s than it is today. It was not thought right to live together without being married. A long period of being single was not something people wanted. It was an uncertain time, and young people wanted to create as much certainty for themselves as possible. Charlotte and I began to talk about what we would do after I was drafted.

My draft notice didn't come until June. I had spent the months since high-school graduation working on the staff at Phyllis Wheatley, picking up a few singing jobs downtown, cleaning after hours at a ladies' shoe shop called the Nicollet Slipper, and wondering what my future held. My brother, Menzy, had been drafted, but didn't leave for an army camp immediately because he was working for the Onan Company, a plant that manufactured small engines needed for the war effort. Menzy made me aware of a possibility I had not considered: I might not qualify for military service because of my polio-weakened right leg.

I was ordered to report for a physical examination at Fort Snelling. I went through that procedure and got the verdict: I was disqualified from regular duty in the armed forces. My leg was too weak. In a way, it was disappointing news. All my friends were going into the military, and I wanted to do my part. But I was also relieved because I did not want to leave Charlotte. I figured, maybe I can be of some good to the war effort here at home. I was informed that I had a choice: find a job in a factory that made war materials or be inducted for what the military called "limited service"—in essence, a corps for the disabled. Defense-plant work sounded more interesting and more promising for the future. Defense-plant work would also keep me in Minneapolis. Several options were close at hand: Honeywell, Minneapolis Moline, International Harvester, Federal Munitions Corporation, and the Onan

Leland Davis Jr., "Menzy," in the U.S. Army in 1943.

Company. Within a day, I applied at all of those places, but my hopes were focused on Onan.

I thought of the Onan Company as a neighbor and a friend. When I was small, a few of us boys would go to Royalston Avenue near our neighborhood to play Tarzan or cowboys and Indians, mimicking our Saturday-afternoon movie heroes. The Onan family owned a house there. When we were playing, D. W. Onan Sr., the founder of the company, would be in his backyard wearing overalls and testing the engines he made. They made a "pop, pop, pop" sound and spewed strange-smelling smoke. He would call to us, "Could you kids please play someplace else while I'm testing this? It can be dangerous." When he was through, he would walk up the street to find us and whistle to get our attention. He would give us each a little Baby Ruth candy bar. We thought that was a great treat.

The small engines Mr. Onan was testing became the basis of his company's declaration as a defense plant. The army wanted his portable power saw and another Onan motor as an electricity generator for its camps. In addition, during the war, Mr. Onan developed an electric igniter for launching rockets from any location. Mr. Onan's company quickly grew to several factory sites, including one where his original garage had been and a much bigger one on Stinson and Broadway Avenues, where Menzy worked as a spray painter.

I talked with my brother about Onan, a company he liked working for. He was the star pitcher on Onan's softball team. He knew the head man at the Stinson Avenue plant, Palmer Stark, and the assistant plant manager, Gene Bursch. Menzy said, "Why don't you come with me to work? I'll take you to see Gene Bursch and Palmer Stark and let them know that you're my brother, that you're looking for a job, and that you were told to get into a defense plant." That's what I did. Gene Bursch interviewed me on the spot and asked me not only about my education and work experience, but also about my ability on the softball field. He invited me to start work on the following Monday, July 6. I would be working in what they called the wash-and-paint department, at fifty cents an hour.

He told me, "You'll work twelve hours a day, five days

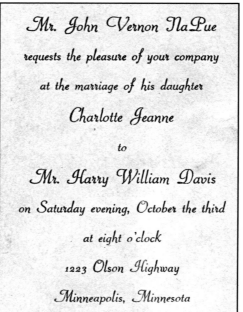

Mr. John Vernon NaPue

requests the pleasure of your company

at the marriage of his daughter

Charlotte Jeanne

to

Mr. Harry William Davis

on Saturday evening, October the third

at eight o'clock

1223 Olson Highway

Minneapolis, Minnesota

Our wedding invitation.

a week." I tried not to let my face show my disappointment at those long hours. Then he seemed to change his mind. "We'll shift that around," he said. "For the day jobs, we need people to work on Saturday, so we're going to shift from the twelve hours a day during the week to ten hours a day, Monday through Friday, and nine hours on Saturday." Either way, those were rough hours, but World War II was on. The Onan plants were running around the clock, six days a week. My job initially was to clean the grease off new engines and generators before they were painted with the army-green paint known as olive-drab. I was to clean them, then take them to the booths where painters would spray them. Mr. Bursch took note of my high-school diploma, which few of his employees had, and decided I could do the painting too.

Menzy would soon help me in another way. He had a 1935 Ford two-door that he sold to me for $300 before he left to serve in the army. I didn't have that kind of money and was too young to sign for a loan, so my mother came to the rescue and signed a loan agreement for me. During the war, gasoline sales to civilians were strictly rationed and many people stopped driving their cars. But because I worked for a defense plant, I could get as much gas as I needed. That solved my transportation problem.

My address changed at about that same time too. I moved in with my mother, in part because she lived right across the street from Charlotte. The second floor of Libby's building included one full apartment, a half-apartment with a kitchen and a bedroom, and one separate bedroom. All of that was shared by my mother, my sister, and my mother's sister, Evelyn Turley. Evelyn's husband, Sam, was in the army's tank corps, based in California. Evelyn had the full apartment, with a bedroom, a living room and dining room combined, and a kitchen. My mother had the half-apartment, and my sister Eva was in the single bedroom. In the fall of 1942, Evelyn wanted to go to California to be with Sam. She proposed that I take over her apartment and buy from her the furniture she did not take along. She offered to let me pay $25 a month for the furniture, with no interest, until it was paid for.

By September, I was a nineteen-year-old high-school graduate with no worries about the draft, a good job, a car, and a furnished apartment. I thought I would make Charlotte NaPue a good husband. That was the proposition I took to her father. Because Charlotte was only sixteen, we needed his written permission to marry.

John NaPue was not crazy about the idea. He depended on Charlotte for help raising her three younger brothers. I pointed out that I coached those boys at Phyllis Wheatley and had a good relationship with them. I would be able to help with them if I joined the family. That won him over. He agreed to the marriage. We also needed my mother's permission, which she gave happily.

We were married on October 3, 1942, in a small evening ceremony in our apartment. The officiating pastor was the Reverend Henry Botts of Zion Baptist, the church I attended while I lived with my sister. My mother, Charlotte's dad, and the few friends who were still around were at the wedding. Afterward, we went to a restaurant, Carver's, on Olson Memorial Highway (Sixth Avenue had just been given that name, in honor of a neighborhood boy, the late Minnesota governor Floyd B. Olson) and had a chicken dinner. There was no honeymoon trip. After dinner,

Charlotte and I were on our way to celebrate our first wedding anniversary when this photo was taken in our car. Our daughter Rita would be born a few weeks later.

we went home. It's hard to imagine a simpler wedding, yet it meant everything to me.

Charlotte and I were ready to create a loving home. After difficult years as teenagers, that is what we both wanted, more than anything. We understood, perhaps better than most young people, the importance of the promises we were making. Some friends said to our faces that they doubted the marriage would last. We celebrated our sixtieth anniversary in 2002. All the people who predicted that our marriage would not last are dead and gone. It's a pity. I'd like to be able to say to those people, "See, I told you!"

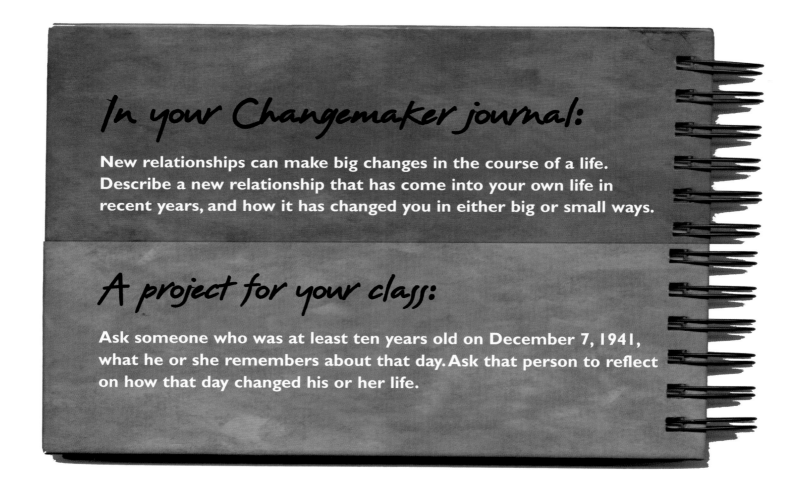

In your Changemaker journal:

New relationships can make big changes in the course of a life. Describe a new relationship that has come into your own life in recent years, and how it has changed you in either big or small ways.

A project for your class:

Ask someone who was at least ten years old on December 7, 1941, what he or she remembers about that day. Ask that person to reflect on how that day changed his or her life.

Working 7

AT THE ONAN COMPANY in 1942, I was in a situation that was new for people of color in Minneapolis. I was working on the line of a factory, side by side with white people who a few years earlier could not imagine working beside a black man. That was the opportunity World War II created. The change came not because white employers were becoming more enlightened, but because they badly needed every worker they could find.

Some of the new black workers in defense plants felt as much discomfort as the white people working alongside them did. But that was not the case with me. I was used to being in situations in which my skin color was different from those around me. Every school I had attended had a mix of black and white students. Through Wheatley athletics, I met white kids from other settlement houses around the city. I knew how to show respect to all people. I began my Onan career determined to have a positive experience.

Onan was a no-nonsense company during the war.

Hours were rigidly observed. Security was tight. Employees had to wear a badge and check in and out with guards every day. Making sure a new worker would fit in was not on the minds of managers, so getting along was up to me. Management's job was to produce the engines and generators that the war required as quickly and flawlessly as possible. Managers were there to give orders and my job was to take orders. It was made clear to me that if I did not comply, they would find someone else for the job. But I was also assured that if I performed well, I would be rewarded with raises and promotion.

My first job was to spray newly assembled engines with degreaser, wipe them clean by hand, and deliver the cleaned product to the spray painters. I became acquainted with people in other departments during lunch hour, when workers ate together and sometimes threw around a ball for fun. But we took our work seriously. We knew if we messed up, we would be out of a job and into the service, somewhere far from our families.

CHANGEMAKER

The Onan Company had a party in June 1943 to celebrate winning an E Award (for excellence) from the U.S. Navy.

It was not long before I renewed my acquaintance with Mr. Onan. One day I was in the rear of the plant in the warehouse, where trucks would back in and unload the biggest generators Onan produced. I was at the controls of a forklift, about to move a big generator, when I heard somebody down the hall say, "Watch it! Watch it! We're coming through." I stopped. There was Mr. Onan. "Hi, Mr. Onan," I said. He said, "Hi, young man. How are you?" I said, "Fine." He said, "Are they working you hard?" I said, "Oh, yes, they do all the time," and he kind of laughed and walked away. After twenty-five or thirty steps, he stopped and strode back to me. "Young man, I know you from somewhere," he said. I said, "I know you too, Mr. Onan." I told him about playing near his house when I was a youngster. He said, "I thought I knew you. Your body has changed, but your face hasn't."

After that day, Mr. Onan made a point of speaking to me every time he came through the plant. He must have asked my managers about me too, because the next time we talked, he knew I had graduated from high school and had taken accounting and bookkeeping. He hinted that my background might be useful to the Onan Company someday.

It must have been a month later when Bud Harr, the foreman, said to me, "We're getting awfully busy, and I'm in charge of the night crew. So I'm going to teach you how to make out the daily reports." I was being promoted to lead man among the spray painters. With my new responsibilities came an extra twenty-five cents an hour. I was up to seventy-five cents an hour. Remember, this was 1943. A top factory wage then was $2 an hour. Plus, that was the wage for the first forty hours. Everything over forty was time-and-a-half, and we were regularly working fifty-four and sixty-hour weeks. So seventy-five cents an hour was a respectable wage for a twenty-year-old. My take-home pay was now about $55 a week. Rent was $20 a month; we were paying off the loan for the car and $25 a month to my aunt for furniture. We were getting by.

I went home all excited and announced, "Charlotte, I got a raise!" The extra money was welcome because Charlotte was pregnant. Our first child, Ritajean Marie, was born October 26, 1943, at Fairview Hospital, the first private hospital in Minneapolis to allow black doctors to practice there. Dr. W. D. Brown, a leader in medicine and civil rights in Minneapolis, delivered Rita. When I saw her for the first time through the window fathers had to peer through in those days, it was such a thrill. What an angel she was! I was so proud, passing out cigars at work the next day.

I had become friendly with my teammates on the Onan softball team, all of whom were a little older than I was. Most were married; some had children; all were white. I was pleased that I blended in well. We had a great time playing softball. Our games were family affairs, with wives and young children coming with picnic suppers to watch the practices and the games.

With Menzy pitching, the Onan-Stinson plant team won the Commercial Blue League, the softball division for teams from midsize companies, two years running. But by the 1943 season, Menzy was in northern Africa, serving with the army quartermaster corps. A year later, he was part of the invasion of Italy. He was sent north through France and got caught in the Battle of the Bulge in the winter of 1944. Fortunately, he came home in one piece. I always believed that his ability to run and jump kept him alive in those dangerous situations.

Even without Menzy, we stayed competitive in our league. But it was when we played softball teams from the other three Onan plants that we had the most fun. Our Onan intramurals concluded each year with an Onan tournament. Mr. Onan and his son Bud would come to watch and cheer, usually for their headquarters plant on Royalston Avenue. But I could always hear Mr. Onan yelling, "Come on, Harry!" when I was up to bat. The University Avenue plant was Onan's biggest and our favorite rival. We beat

them all the time. Our Stinson managers would get a bet going against the other plant managers. Those bets would often involve the purchase of beer for the team after the game.

One night after a softball game, plant manager Gene Bursch invited the whole Stinson-plant team to join him for a beer at the Streamline Café and Bar on Broadway Avenue. It was a good-sized place, popular

My brother, Menzy, was the star pitcher on the Onan-Stinson plant softball team before he was called up for military service.

with the Onan crowd. I never liked to drink, but this time, to be sociable, I decided to have a beer with my teammates. Gene ordered a round of beers for the whole team. The waiter came back with beer for everybody except me.

Gene noticed what had happened. "Harry, you didn't get your beer yet?" he said loudly, so the waiter would hear. I said no. Then he hollered at the bartender, "Hey! We've got another ballplayer over here. Where's the beer for him?" "We don't serve him" was the answer. Gene said, "What do you mean, you don't serve him?" He said,

"No, we don't serve Negroes." That got a rise out of Gene. "Do you mean to tell me that you won't serve this young man, whose brother is over fighting for your freedom, who works in our defense plant, which is supplying the material for the army?" The bartender said, "No, my boss told me not to." He said, "You tell your boss that Gene Bursch of the Onan Company is going to file a complaint with the city of Minneapolis."

He did just that, with the full backing of Mr. Onan. A few days later, I got a call from someone in the front office, telling me to come to a meeting in Mr. Onan's office. The owner of the Streamline Café was present with his lawyer. They had come to apologize in person, to deliver a letter of apology, and to pay me a modest sum of money. I cannot remember how much it was, so it must have been small. But I will never forget that apology and how good it made me feel. Charlotte's reaction, though, also says something about the fear black people lived with in those years. She was afraid that somehow, someday, the Streamline people would retaliate against me.

By 1945, I was happily settled at Onan and content to stay there for a long time. Of course, I knew that the United States was winning the war, but even after victory was declared in Europe in May, all of us expected fighting against the Japanese—and the military's demand for Onan engines—to continue for some time. We were astonished at news of the atomic-bomb attacks on Hiroshima August 6 and Nagasaki August 9, and the swift end of the war less than two weeks later.

I thought that with three years of service, my job was secure. My foreman, Bud Harr, told me as much. I don't know who was more surprised, Bud or me, when my name appeared on the layoff list a few months after the fighting ended. Bud insisted that a mistake had been made and that he would set it right. But there was no mistake. The problem was that jobs were owed to fellows who had been Onan employees before the war and who had been away in the service, fellows like my brother. The law required that returning servicemen could claim their old jobs. Bud himself was affected. Instead of continuing as a foreman at the Stinson plant, he wound up at the University Avenue plant, demoted from foreman to lead man. He vowed to keep his eye out for an opening for me to return to Onan. But in his new role, he couldn't do much on my behalf.

Suddenly, my sideline job coaching boxing at Phyllis Wheatley was my only job. After my layoff, Phyllis Wheatley matched the $35 a month that the *Star* and *Tribune* paid me and gave me a part-time staff position. But $70 a month would not cut it. Not with a two-year-old in the family and another baby on the way. Our son Harry William, whom we call Butch, was born April 15, 1946.

One opportunity I had to make more money was to train my better young boxers for professional careers. I would sometimes go down to Potts Gym at Sixth and Hennepin, over the old Aster Theater, to work out. That was where the local boxers who had turned professional trained, and where promoters would come to recruit new talent. I knew that promoters would pay me to coach boxers into the professional ranks. But through my Uncle Dixie, I also knew that gangsters often tried to control professional boxers and their managers, and would threaten honest ones who didn't want to play along. That made me afraid of getting involved.

Boxing connections landed me another job. A regular fan at any local boxing match was Reuben Bloom, a car dealer. He used to sit at ringside during matches. One day, we struck up a conversation. He said, "Harry, where do you work?" I explained that I had recently been laid off at Onan. He said, "I own Broadway Motors." It was a DeSoto-Plymouth dealer on Broadway and James Avenues in north Minneapolis. "Why don't you come up and see me? I'll give you a job. What can you do?" I told him I could do anything—wash cars, grease cars, undercoat cars, put on car-seat covers. I went the next day and was hired to do all the things I had mentioned to Reub and more.

Finances were still tight at home, so I started one more moneymaking activity on the side: a home-maintenance service. A friend named Harry Miller and I painted our names on the side of a little red pickup truck and went into business doing household jobs for people who could afford such a service. We were busy in the spring and fall of 1946 and 1947, taking down and putting up storm windows on large houses.

Between that business and my work at Broadway Motors and Phyllis Wheatley, I was keeping groceries on the table at home. I was busy, maybe busier than a father with young children should be. That's why I was pleased with the news Charlotte had for me one fall day in 1948 when I came home for lunch: she had received a phone call from the Onan Company. When I returned the call, I was invited to meet with Jack Shea, an Onan vice president. He had a job for me at Onan's University Avenue plant, one of the two plants the company still operated after postwar downsizing. I was to be a spray painter again. But I was offered $1.50 an hour—fifty cents a hour more than I had been making at Broadway Motors—plus health insurance for me and my family, plus a promise: after six months, I would be a junior foreman. And I would receive training that might someday let me leave the dirty-coverall, menial tasks I had been doing and become a manager in a shirt and tie. I took the Onan job.

My new foreman in the wash-and-paint department and the finish-paint department was Ralph Markwood. Within about four weeks of rejoining the Onan Company, I became Ralph's junior foreman. I had a desk and a phone, right in the middle of the production areas. I would receive calls informing our department how many of which items were coming through and on what schedule. I would then assign the pieces to the lead man in each department for processing. It was a juggling act I got pretty good at performing.

I received my twenty-year watch from the Onan Company in 1965. The man in shirtsleeves is CEO Bud Onan, the son of the company's founder.

I joined the Onan Chorus in the early 1950s and sang baritone with the group until I left the company in 1968. I am in the first row, on the far left.

Unfortunately, no matter how well I did my job, it seemed that I could not please my foreman. Not long after I became junior foreman, Ralph played a role in getting my brother Menzy fired. A disagreement had erupted in the finishing department, where Menzy worked. Ralph blamed Menzy for the conflict—unfairly, in my opinion—and went to the personnel department with a recommendation that Menzy be dismissed.

When a new automated conveyor system came into our department, Ralph resented my efforts to learn as much as I could about its operation. He would snap at me in anger when I tried to become more familiar with it. After several days of that treatment, I worked up my courage to say to him, "Ralph, I'm a grown man just like you are. I was trained in this just like you were. If you will talk to me like I'm a man, then I don't think we'll have any problems."

That exchange may have cleared the air for the moment, but the tension between us steadily got worse. Ralph seemed jealous of the success of my Golden Gloves teams. He frowned whenever he saw a member of the Onan family speaking to me. He didn't appreciate my involvement in the Onan Chorus, a men's group that sang at all the company events and performed in competition at the Minneapolis Aquatennial. We won that competition several years running and were flown in the company plane to Chicago for the Chicago Musicland Festival. We won that contest too!

I don't want to suggest that the problem between Ralph and me was entirely his fault. It was a two-way street. I had trouble forgiving him for what happened to Menzy. He may have had reason to dislike me. People in the plant often bypassed him and came to me with questions, and I may have encouraged them to do that.

In 1965, Ralph made a move to get rid of me. He went to Jerry Olson in the personnel office and said he could no longer tolerate me as his junior foreman, offering some trumped-up reason why I should be fired. I was told later that Jerry said, "Ralph, I can't do that. He's respected by the Onan family, and, incidentally, he's done an outstanding job." From what I understand, Ralph's move started a series of conversations among Onan executives about my future.

Not long after Ralph's complaint, I was called into the personnel department to meet with the director, Ralph Hanson. He said, "Harry, Ralph has asked that you be removed as a junior foreman." I said, "Does that mean I'm going to get fired?" He said, "We have nothing to fire you for." He told me that if I were interested in leaving the paint department, I could have another position in the company: head of employee services. It was the position in charge of employee activities, including men's and women's sports, the Onan Chorus, companywide picnics and events, and a variety of service projects involving employees. It was a management job. I could wear a shirt and tie to work, just as I had always wanted. I happily accepted and became the first black employee to move into a white-collar position at the Onan Company.

In your Changemaker journal:

Describe a time when you or someone you know well had trouble getting along with someone. What attempt was made to improve the situation? What other action might have been taken? What would you recommend doing if all attempts at improving the relationship failed, as Harry Davis's did with his foreman, Ralph Markwood?

Coaching 8

BY THE EARLY 1940s, boxing had become a required part of the Phyllis Wheatley Settlement House program for boys. Ray Hatcher believed boxing taught boys discipline, self-control, anger management, confidence, and strength. It prepared them to defend themselves if necessary. Those were lessons he thought were important for black boys growing up in white Minneapolis.

But as important as boxing was at the Wheatley, the program operated for years without a head coach. War reduced the number of men in our neighborhood. I was an assistant coach who had no head coach to report to.

As fall 1943 approached, the new Phyllis Wheatley director, Henry Thomas, knew he had to find a head coach for the program to survive. He found me. He said, "Harry, would you be willing to coach? The *Star Journal* will pay you $35 a month. We've organized the program. You know all the kids." Indeed I did. I was also a new father. Volunteering for little or no pay was losing its appeal, but serious coaching, for a paycheck big enough to cover my monthly car payment and gasoline costs, sounded good. I accepted Henry's offer.

By then, the Golden Gloves network of newspaper-sponsored youth boxing programs stretched around the country. It was popular and well organized in our Northwest Division. Seasons would begin in the fall and wind up in early February with a city tournament, in mid-February with the Northwest divisional tournament, and in early March with a national tournament. The city and divisional events always took place in the Minneapolis Auditorium; national tournaments were in Chicago. At its peak, the Northwest Golden Gloves program involved several thousand boys every year.

At Phyllis Wheatley, I had about 125 young boxers at a time to coach. Five days a week, I would come to the Wheatley at six o'clock and start the evening's round of classes. I had a one-hour class for each group of boxers. There were three groups the first years and four later on. The Junior Golden Gloves were boys ages ten to fourteen.

Then came the B Class, the sixteen- to twenty-year-olds; that group was later split in two. The Open Class took in experienced young men, ages twenty to twenty-two.

I discovered quickly that I could not give 125 kids the attention it takes to develop individual skills in each one. So I developed a handbook that described different boxing styles. I then assigned small groups of kids to use the handbook as they practiced a particular style for a given period. The groups would rotate so each boy would be exposed to a variety of styles. Further, I assigned each of the Open Class boxers to be the trainer for a small group of younger boxers. Each of the top fighters would have four or five Junior Golden Gloves and four or five B Class fighters to supervise per night. I would supervise the Open Class fighters as they worked with the younger boys in the early part of the evening. Then after the youngsters went home, I would give the top fighters individual instruction. I helped each boxer develop a boxing style that was right for him.

I found myself mentally returning to the boxing instruction I had received from my Uncle Dixie when I was eleven or twelve and copying it in the lessons I set up. He had been patient with me, teaching me all the basic skills in sequence. We worked a great deal on stance. He would compare a boxer's stances with those of baseball players. Have you ever noticed the way a long-ball hitter places his feet for stability and power, and compared that stance with that of the base-hitter who needs to spring quickly

down the first-base line? My uncle had me doing that kind of analysis of every move I made in the ring. He also concentrated on leverage. Only a few fighters have a natural ability to be strong punchers. Everybody else has to learn the trick of maximizing a punch through leverage, which means throwing one's weight into a punch without losing balance. We went over and over these things that summer he trained me. Repetition, I learned, is an important part of teaching.

I remembered those lessons. When I tried them myself as a coach, I discovered anew how effective they were. So I wrote them down and assembled them into a coaching manual. It was a book not just for me but for all the Open Class boxers I assigned to work with younger kids. Of course, by teaching, they were learning. So was I.

I had few Open Class fighters those first years. But beginning in the fall of 1945, their numbers swelled, until I had twenty or twenty-five boxers per year in the Open Class. In 1945 I was the same age as some of them, just twenty-two. But I had been coaching for four years and had no trouble winning their respect.

I came to understand that teaching was my true sports talent—my calling, one might say. I was a much better teacher than boxer. I focused not only on what to teach but how to teach it. I had always admired good teachers, and I came to realize that what I had actually learned from them was how to teach.

I took coaching seriously, partly because it provided

extra income that Charlotte and I needed as our family grew. But more than money was involved. Coaching inspired me. It made me think about what it means to be an adult and to influence young lives. I became a father just as I started coaching. I wanted to be the best coach I possibly could be so that I could teach both my own children and the boxers how to be winners. What I discovered was that coaching was fathering too. Most of the boys I worked with either had no father or a busy and distracted father. Families in our neighborhood were large and

poor, and fathers often worked a number of jobs. I was well aware that I was supplying some male guidance that my boxers might not receive otherwise. I had a sense that a lot of my boys were looking for someone to tell them how to live. I could say to them, "You are somebody."

I adopted the lesson that Ray Hatcher taught: Successful living has three components—body, mind, and spirit. That idea became the cornerstone of my coaching. Your body is your temple, I told the boys, yours to use or abuse. If you abuse it, it won't be in good working order when you need it. They would say, "What do you mean?" I would tell them about matches I had seen involving boxers who had been drunk the night before. They would enter the ring cocksure they could win and would fail miserably. That's what comes from not taking care of one's body, I would say.

To emphasize that point, we began the program by building the boys' physical fitness. We put them through a routine of calisthenics and weight lifting before we started working on boxing skills. I had them do push-ups on their fingers, not their whole hands, to strengthen their hands against injuries. Exercises to build up the neck muscles were part of the routine to better enable the neck to withstand punches. Balance, footwork, and timing are crucial in boxing, so much so that we included ballet instruction in the program. The lady who taught arts at Phyllis Wheatley would bring a few of her ballet students to the gym and have them demonstrate ballet moves. Younger

The stars of the Wheatley 1953–1954 boxing team (from left): Ray Wells, Charles Smith, and Neil Frazier. Ray became my kinsman when he married my first cousin, Rene Jackson; Neil Frazier went on to be a bishop in the Church of God and Christ.

kids would laugh at big boxers doing ballet. I would say, "You join the class and I'll show you how the boys you were laughing at have the advantage over you, just for dancing."

Only after improving the boys' fitness would we start teaching boxing fundamentals. We gave each punch a number so we could teach combinations of punches as a sequence of numbers and instruct the boys to vary that sequence by changing the numbers. Only after all those punches were mastered did we begin to work on an individual style for each boxer.

In addition to coaching boxing at Phyllis Wheatley, I also coached football for ten-year-olds. The player in the center of the back row was future Minneapolis school superintendent Richard Green.

All the while, I was telling the boys that their minds are in control of their bodies. The mind learns the lessons and acquires the skills that make a person competent. That's where confidence comes from. Confidence is the by-product of knowing what you need to know. I tried to make boxers think about the mental work required for good performance. For example, I might say to a boy in the middle of a practice bout, "Here's the combination I want you to throw. Remember, we practiced that? Now I'm going to see if you've got confidence in yourself." I was always trying to offer more than a physical challenge, to show them that there is more to life than physical ability.

I also talked about the spirit. I believe that a relationship with God adds a vital dimension to life: meaning. Knowing God and that God loves you is a powerful force for good in a young life. It gives a boy reason to take care of his mind and his body. He understands them as gifts from God. I wanted my boxers to want to live moral, upright lives and to know they are beloved children of God.

But I also wanted the boys who did not have an internal spiritual compass to be guided by some firm rules. I had only had a few: No drinking. No smoking. No drugs. Do any of those things, I said, and you put yourself out of

Eddie Lacy was the first Upper Midwest Golden Gloves champion my Phyllis Wheatley team produced. He started winning championships in 1945.

contention. No skipping practice without a real excuse. If you miss a session without an excuse, you go "on penalty." That meant a boxer was required to do one of two things. If you were a senior boxer, you would have to box an extra round, without stopping, against a fresh opponent. That may sound easy, but, believe me, it is not. If the offender was too young yet to be boxing, he would have to do an extra series of push-ups or sit-ups or an extra round of rope-skipping. I made my rules stick, even with my champions. In 1955 and 1956, Willie Jemison won championships. He decided the next year that he needed to show up at practice only when it suited him, which was not often enough. When the 1957 tournament began, he needed an entry blank signed by me to compete. I refused to sign. A boxer he used to spar with won that year.

I took one more page from Ray Hatcher's book when I told the boys one night, "We've got something special planned. You are going to put on a boxing exhibition—at Stillwater state penitentiary." That visit helped the boys understand that obeying the rules was important not only in boxing but in life.

It was important to me to teach my boxers to respect themselves, each other, their opponents, and the adults in their lives. So even when I was not much older than some of the boxers, I asked them to call me Mr. Davis. They called their schoolteachers Mister, and I wanted them to consider me at a teacher's level of authority. I also insisted that they address the referees at a match as Mister. I instructed them to make eye contact as they listened to the referee giving instructions and respond with "Yes, sir," and no back talk. One custom I started has carried over into Olympic boxing: I taught my boxers to bow to the judges after the bout. That caught on as a show of courtesy and respect and is widely practiced today.

I set high standards of conduct for myself too. I said to my teams, "Some coaches say, 'Don't do as I do. Do as I say.' I say, 'Do as I say, and watch me to make sure that I do as I say too.' I won't smoke. I won't drink. I won't miss training days. I'm going through the same discipline you are." I wasn't making a big change in my habits. I had never been much of a drinker and only smoked a few times to be sociable during breaks at the Onan plant. That was before Americans learned how damaging smoking is to one's health. By the time that hazard was known, I had sworn off cigarettes for good. The only time I would miss a training day was when Charlotte was giving birth. My teams allowed me that one excuse for an absence.

The best thing I did to persuade my boxers to respect me was to win. We won our first Golden Gloves tournament in 1945, starting a winning tradition that would last all my years as boxing coach at Phyllis Wheatley. Boys who wanted to be winners gravitated to my program.

A scrappy, skinny kid named Eddie Lacy became our program's first Upper Midwest Golden Gloves champion. He was really gifted. He was about thirteen, little, and frail when he first started boxing at Phyllis Wheatley in 1943. He didn't have much of a father figure in his life, other than an older brother. He came from a poor family. We used to have the Wheatley housekeeper find clothes for him. But what a fast learner! He

could box, he could counterpunch, and he was faster than greased lightning. He had what boxers call natural leverage. He could move in any direction without losing his balance. He was a respectful kid who never used foul language, never smoked, and always tried to help younger kids. He boxed in the flyweight division—that's 112 pounds—in 1945. (In those years there were eight weight divisions in boxing: flyweight, bantamweight, featherweight, lightweight, welterweight, middleweight, light heavyweight, and heavyweight. Now, there are twelve divisions: light

From left: Danny Davis, Wes Hayden, Johnny Bible, and Roger Frazier prepare with me for "Onan Nite" at the Upper Midwest Golden Gloves 1951 tournament. Onan sponsored a night at the tournament every year after my teams became successful. These four boxers all became Onan employees at some point during the 1950s; each went on to fine careers.

flyweight, flyweight, bantamweight, featherweight, light-weight, junior welterweight, welterweight, junior middle-weight, middleweight, light heavyweight, heavyweight, and super heavyweight.) The professional boxers who trained at Potts Gym downtown sometimes asked me to bring Eddie there to spar with them, that's how good he was.

In 1948, Eddie and another outstanding fighter, Danny Davis, led us to our first Upper Midwest team championship and put in a strong performance at the Golden Gloves national tournament. Buddy Bunn and Roland Johnson were also strong fighters that year, as was the 1949 city heavyweight champion, Cozelle Breedlove. He went on to be executive director at Phyllis Wheatley in the 1980s.

I accompanied Golden Gloves star flyweight Jimmy Jackson on the Hiawatha train to Chicago for the 1957 national Golden Gloves tournament.

That first Upper Midwest team championship won me the right to accompany our athletes to Chicago for the national Golden Gloves tournament. Also along were *Star* and *Tribune* sportswriters Charlie Johnson and George Barton. They stayed at the Palmer House down-town, while my black boxers and I were relegated to the Parkway Hotel in a bad part of town. It was so rough that most taxi drivers would not go there. We got very little sleep there because there was so much activity all night long. After a couple of nights of this, I had had enough. I announced to Charlie Johnson, "Either we stay at the Pal-mer House or we go back to Minneapolis on the next train." It was not usual for black people to stay at the Palmer House in those years, but somehow Charlie got us in.

We had a similar scene in Kansas City, Missouri, when Charlie and I accompanied a few of our boxers to the Amateur Athletic Union national tournament in 1948. Our group included two white boxers, Danny Dillon and Vince Donnelly; two blacks, Danny Davis and Eddie Lacy; and one Latino, Johnny Pacheco. When we arrived at the famous Muehlebach Hotel in Kansas City, the registration clerk refused to provide rooms for Danny Davis, Eddie, Johnny, and me. This time Charlie took the initiative. He com-plained loudly, got the hotel manager involved, invoked the fact that the hotel admitted colored U.S. servicemen, and got us in. We learned afterward that other black boxers in the same tournament had been shunted off to a terrible hotel. We performed well in that tournament, with two national championships and three runners-up. I maintain that getting a good night's sleep helped us win.

Wheatley teams started winning the city's team championships consistently in 1951, the year we had three divisional champs and one runner-up. We won city team championships through the remainder of the 1950s and won seven team championships at the Upper Midwest division level during that decade.

There were so many outstanding boxers on Wheatley teams during those years that I hesitate to begin naming them. But, with advance apologies to those I omit, I have to mention Jimmy Jackson and some of his teammates. Jimmy won Upper Midwest championships in the flyweight division every year from 1954 to 1959 and won the national Golden Gloves title in 1957. Jimmy was the soft-spoken star of a team of outstanding athletes that included heavyweight Jerry Bailey, light heavyweight LeRoy Bogar, bantamweights Kenny Rodriguez and Chuck Hales, and welterweight Jimmy Shaw. Each of those young men rose through the Phyllis Wheatley ranks from boyhood—all except Hales, who grew up in Staples, a small central-Minnesota town. As a high-school kid, he was one of the Upper Midwest winners I took on our divisional team to national tournaments. He joined the Wheatley team after he graduated from high school. In fact, he moved to the Twin Cities because he wanted to train with me.

Some of those men were present at a boxers reunion at Phyllis Wheatley in May 2001. It was good to hear them reminisce with this book's editor about their years on Wheatley boxing teams. Jimmy Jackson said that what motivated him and his teammates to succeed was the sense that "Harry really cared about us—every individual. He really wanted us to succeed and to develop our skills." Chuck Hales said, "He could calm you down when you were boxing in front of ten thousand people. He was someone you could draw strength from." Ken Rodriguez said, "He was like a father to us."

In 1959, Phyllis Wheatley's gym was host to the city Golden Gloves tournament. That was an honor for us and a lot of responsibility. I organized more than one hundred volunteers to prepare for and run the tournament. We repainted the gym, installed new bleachers, published a special program, and performed many last-minute tasks. D. W. Onan donated the expensive team trophies.

That tournament turned out to be something of a last hurrah for me as a Golden Gloves coach. The administrator's position at Star Tribune Charities, the parent organization of the Upper Midwest Golden Gloves, became open that year. I was asked about my interest in the job. It would be a part-time position with a modest salary, but a larger sum than I was earning as a coach. Money was an issue for us in those years, with college just ahead for Rita and Butch. Charlotte and I were moonlighting to make more money, cleaning the Flameburger restaurant every night between 10:00 and midnight.

Before long, I was summoned to a meeting at Charlie

Johnson's office at the newspaper. He made the offer official. I asked for a few days to think it over and talk with my Golden Gloves boxers. It wasn't an easy decision; I felt very attached to the kids I coached. But my boxers encouraged me to take the job. I think it was Jimmy Jackson who said, "Harry, then you can quit that cleaning job down at the Flameburger." I had always prepared a few of the older boxers to be leaders so that they could take charge if something happened to me. Among them was Ray Wells. He was ready to succeed me as coach. With

that in mind, I accepted Charlie's offer.

In 1963, I received the George Barton Award for making the greatest contribution to boxing in Minnesota, bestowed by a group of boxing fans called the Old Guards of the Ring. Dick Cullum wrote about the award for the *Tribune,* saying, "Nowhere in the country is amateur boxing more intelligently and carefully supervised than in Harry Davis' realm. . . . Moreover, no coach had more respect, admiration and downright affection for his boys." The feeling was mutual, and it lingers to this day.

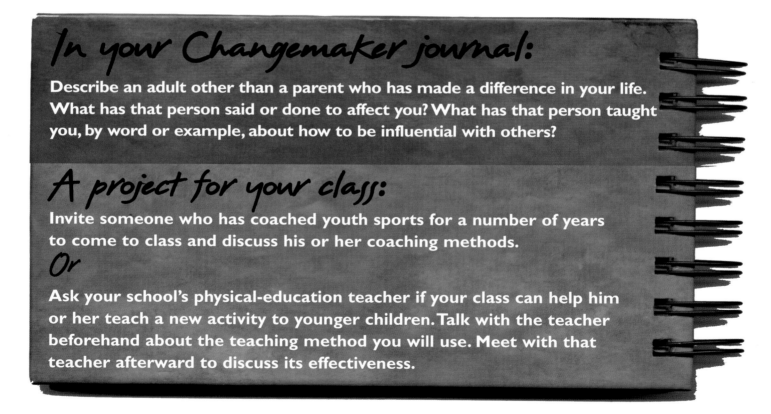

In your Changemaker journal:

Describe an adult other than a parent who has made a difference in your life. What has that person said or done to affect you? What has that person taught you, by word or example, about how to be influential with others?

A project for your class:

Invite someone who has coached youth sports for a number of years to come to class and discuss his or her coaching methods.

Or

Ask your school's physical-education teacher if your class can help him or her teach a new activity to younger children. Talk with the teacher beforehand about the teaching method you will use. Meet with that teacher afterward to discuss its effectiveness.

Nurturing

SOME YOUNG PEOPLE MARRY to escape their families. For Charlotte and me, it seemed that just the opposite happened. We became more involved with our families after we married and had a family of our own.

The apartment on Olson Highway that seemed so perfect for Charlotte and me in 1942 seemed much too small less than a year later, when we were expecting the birth of our first child. We moved into the upper level of a duplex at 1106 Emerson, which was next door to a box factory and across the street from the downstairs duplex where my sister Dooney and her family lived. A few years later, conscious of the fire hazard posed by the box factory, we moved into the unit above Dooney's apartment. I was once again close to my eldest sister.

At 1107 Emerson, we made a home for Charlotte's three younger brothers for a time. Her father couldn't find the help he needed to care for the boys as they reached their teen years. They were close to Charlotte, who had been their second mother, and to me, through Phyllis

Wheatley activities. Her dad trusted us to care for them. We did, though under very crowded conditions. Eventually, Charlotte's uncle took the boys into his home. The youngest boy, Vern, was with us longer than the others, Delmar and Donald.

Living close to Dooney meant that I again saw my own father occasionally. He stayed closer to Dooney than to the rest of his children after he and my mother separated. He paid Dooney to care for me during my high-school years, and I seldom saw him then, not even at my athletic or musical performances. He nearly disappeared from my life for several years. But after our children were born, Dad occasionally visited us. Slowly, we began to have a more regular relationship. Sometimes, he would pop up suddenly. One year, when I was sitting at the head table of our boxing team's postseason appreciation banquet, I looked up and was surprised to see Dad walk in. A few other times, after my name had been in the paper in connection with Golden Gloves, he would appear at a practice

My mother was in poor health when the family gathered for this photo in about 1958. Standing (from left): Joyce, the cousin my mother raised; Leland Jr. "Menzy"; Charlotte "Dooney"; and I. Seated (from left): Eva; my mother, Libby; and Geraldine.

or a match, sit down, and talk with me. I knew that he was following my achievements and that he was proud of me. Dad lived a long life, reaching age eighty-three before dying in 1970.

My mother was not blessed with as many years, but I enjoyed a better relationship with her than with my father. She was a great help to Charlotte after the birth of our babies. She was a regular babysitter for Rita, whom she called "Peaches" because of her round little cheeks, and for Butchie. She participated often in Phyllis Wheatley activities and followed my boxing teams. She was a cook

for the mothers' group at the Wheatley. She maintained her own little apartment and lived quite independently as she grew older. She died in 1958 at age sixty.

The other relative from my parents' generation who made a big difference in my life, Uncle Dixie, stayed in touch with me through my young adulthood. After his professional boxing days were done and his brief first marriage ended, Uncle Dixie settled in Minneapolis. He remained athletic, so much so that he would run downtown and back. He used to go to restaurants on Washington Avenue in the years when that street was getting a bad reputation. He wasn't afraid of a tough neighborhood. Once, when he was in his seventies, a couple of fellows jumped him as he came out of a restaurant. They didn't know he was a former boxer, and he got the better of them in the tussle. As a result, Uncle Dixie was arrested and had to appear before a judge. The arresting officer testified, "These two young men were beaten up by this man." The judge asked my uncle, "How old are you?" He told them he was seventy-something. The judge asked, "Mr. Davis, what did they do to provoke you?" He said, "They were trying to rob me. They jumped me because I'm an old man. I defended myself. I'm a former prizefighter." The judge dismissed the case.

Uncle Dixie was a big fan of my Golden Gloves teams. He would come to the Upper Midwest championships at the Minneapolis Auditorium. If I spotted him, I would invite him to sit with me at ringside. He enjoyed that special treatment. Since Uncle Dixie had no children of his own, I became like a son to him. He always smiled to hear me tell people, "This is the guy who taught me how to box." Uncle Dixie died at age seventy-seven.

The other father figure in my life was my brother, Menzy. Nine years older and without any children of his own, Menzy took a great interest in me and, later, my children. Though Menzy did not graduate from high school himself—neither had my sisters—he encouraged me to get a good education. He liked to give me advice, the way a father would. He would say, "Pops, if you're going to do something, you're going to have to decide that you will have competence in doing it. You need to think, 'I can do this better than anybody.'" That was the attitude he took to the pitcher's mound and the batter's box when he played baseball. I often thought that if he had gone to high school, he would have become a professional ballplayer. Menzy died at age sixty-seven, in 1982.

Of course, my most important relationships were with Charlotte and our children. Charlotte and I had the great advantage of sharing common values. We both were raised by mothers who cared deeply for their children and lived by similar principles. We both had grown up under the strong influences of the Minneapolis Public Schools, our neighborhood churches, and Phyllis Wheatley's Gertrude Brown. After our marriage, we worked at developing common interests and activities while at the same time respecting each other's differences. Charlotte was

not much interested in boxing, but she supported what I did there. She would bring the children down to watch practices, but then she and Rita would stray over into the girls' department at the Wheatley, while Butchie stayed to watch me. That was as it should be, I thought.

Charlotte didn't go back to school after our marriage, but she did go to work, as a retail sales clerk. She worked for Sears briefly before Rita was born. Then, a few years after Butch arrived, she went to work for the city's most prestigious department store, Dayton's. Charlotte was among the first black women to hold such a position; downtown-Minneapolis department stores did not hire their first black employees until 1948. Charlotte was good at her job, and she is still. She still works part-time today as a clothing-store clerk, and her services are much in demand.

Becoming parents cemented the love Charlotte and I share. The day she told me she was pregnant was one of the great days of my life. It started a new chapter for me. Even though we had been behaving like adults, it seemed as though we did not really become adults until we were parents. From the moment I knew that Charlotte was expecting, I began to think of myself as responsible for young lives. I thought, it's up to me to put groceries on the table, clothes on their backs, and pillows under their heads. I have to give them love and attention. I have to look after more than just their earthly needs.

Rita was a bright, affectionate child with a strong

personality. Even as a tyke, she knew how to speak her mind. When I came home from work, I loved the attention she would give me. She could boss me and get anything she wanted, or so Charlotte claimed.

Charlotte and I began to think about Rita's education when she was barely a toddler. We vowed, "We will never give our children to any school system. We will go to school with them. We will learn along with them." We promised each other that when we took our children to kindergarten, both of us would take them. We would become acquainted with the teacher and know the principal. We would keep up with the work that they were doing.

We kept our promise and went with Rita to Grant School, just one block north and two short blocks west of our duplex on Eleventh and Emerson. Three years later, Butchie followed her there. We got to know their teachers, all of whom were white. They took a sincere interest in Rita and Butch. Grant School had an active Parent-Teacher Association, which we joined, though I admit that Charlotte took the lead there because of the demands of my Golden Gloves schedule.

Of course, both Rita and Butch attended nursery school at Phyllis Wheatley. When Charlotte was working and Butch was four or five and in nursery school, Rita—who was just three years older—would walk down Eleventh Avenue to Aldrich and then down Aldrich to Eighth Avenue to take Butchie to nursery school in the morning. Then she would come all the way back and go to Grant School. She learned responsibility early and handled it well.

We had a dog that we called Poodle, though he was a yellow Lab. He was a valued member of the family. We lived on a busy street that always seemed to be bustling with children as well as cars. When he was outside with Rita or Butch, Poodle would walk along the curb as if he were patrolling. If any of the kids would head toward the street, he would walk between them and the street, seemingly trying to herd them back. He was a favorite of the neighborhood children. They could do anything to him—pull his ears or his tail or lay on him—and he would never growl or snap. But if any adult came over to the children while they were playing, he would look the person over. If the person didn't look familiar, he would show his teeth.

The store next door sold fish. The fishmonger would cut off the fish heads and throw them into the garbage. One day, I noticed a terrible smell in the children's bedroom. Before long, we all were saying, "Gee, something stinks in that room!" Finally, we found a fish head in Rita's doll buggy under some doll blankets. She assured us that she had not brought any such thing into the house. The culprit must have been Poodle.

Our home was important to us, and we worked hard to make it nice, even though we had no chance of owning it. We painted the place, upgraded the oil stove, and bought linoleum for the kitchen floor. It was cozy, but with just two bedrooms we were crowded.

After I went back to work for the Onan Company in 1948, we began to think about something our parents could only dream about: buying a home. After World War II, lenders began to be willing to give black people the loans, or mortgages, needed to buy homes in a few Minneapolis neighborhoods. We knew if we could save for a down payment, we had a fair chance of persuading a lender to help us buy a house. We didn't have much money. As a junior foreman at Onan in the early 1950s, I made $1.95 an hour. But I made a little more coaching and Charlotte made a little more at her job. We were working hard, but we were young and had a dream that energized us.

Our serious house-hunting began in 1953. Charlotte held out hope that we could find a home for sale on the North Side, but that neighborhood's housing stock was deteriorating in those years. Some of the nicer homes, those with hardwood floors and pretty banisters, had been torn down. All the places we liked were too expensive for us. Discouraged, we stopped looking for a time and saved more money.

We were resigned to leaving the North Side when we resumed house hunting in 1954. We were also increasingly desperate for more room. That summer, Charlotte was pregnant with our third child, Richard Charles (we call him Ricky), who would be born on February 7, 1955. The Central High School neighborhood seemed the right place to look. South of downtown Minneapolis, Central was the part of the city where middle-class black people had lived for more than a generation. Men with the best jobs available to blacks in those years—Pullman porters, postal workers, streetcar drivers, hotel workers—settled with their families in the Central area. The neighborhood was dominated by small, bungalow-style single-family homes, selling then for about $15,000. For us, that was not an impossible reach.

We found what we were seeking at 3621 Portland Avenue South. It was a three-bedroom bungalow in the middle of the block on a busy street. It was a sound, well-kept stucco house with a fenced yard, front and back. But what we really appreciated was its closeness to three schools—Warrington, the elementary school; Bryant, the junior high school; and Central High School. All were considered among the city's best in the 1950s. Sadly, all of them are gone today.

We told ourselves that we weren't really leaving the North Side, because we stayed active at Phyllis Wheatley. By then, Rita was eleven and Butchie was eight. Before long, we considered them old enough to take the bus to the Wheatley. Butch played football there and Rita took classes. We also felt that we were not among strangers on the South Side; many friends our age from the old neighborhood had already moved south.

What we did not fully grasp at the time was that we were part of the breakup of what had been the Minneapolis ghetto. The North Side of our childhood was home to blacks and Jews, joined by the fact that they were not welcome to live anywhere else in Minneapolis. When other parts of the city opened to blacks and Jews in the 1950s, the middle-class members of the old neighborhood moved out. Those of us who moved landed in nicer, safer neighborhoods. But we lost something too: we would never again experience the close neighborly feeling we grew up with. The bigger losers, though, were the people left behind, many of them quite poor. Those of us who moved away took with us a lot of the resources needed to make a neighborhood strong.

We found our house in Central when some friends told us about it and suggested that we take a look. We piled Rita and Butch into the car and set out to just drive by, but when we stopped the car to give it a long look, the older lady who owned it called to us, "Would you like to come in?" She introduced herself as Mrs. Nanna Estelle, and she could not have been more gracious. She explained that she was a retired nurse, originally from Sweden, and that she had decided to move back to Sweden to be near family in her declining years. She took a great interest in us and in our children, and gave us a chatty tour of the house. We liked its oil-burning furnace, its three-season porch, and—a first for us—its partially finished basement. We also liked Mrs. Estelle. She could see that Charlotte was pregnant, and she treated her in a motherly way.

We were sold on the house, but we were concerned about being able to get a mortgage to cover the $12,000 asking price. We went to a downtown institution we had heard about when we were kids, Farmers and Mechanics Bank. Schoolchildren in Minneapolis in the 1930s were given the opportunity to start savings accounts at Farmers and Mechanics by making deposits every Friday, right at school. The idea was to teach us the habit of saving money. It also left us with a friendly feeling toward that bank. Our confidence in F & M was rewarded, though it helped that Mrs. Estelle came down a little in her asking price. We got a mortgage for $9,000.

Only a few months separated our move and Ricky's arrival. His timing was an early indication of his attention-getting personality. He was born on the night of the semifinal bouts in the 1955 Golden Gloves Upper Midwest tournament. It was a year when we had an outstanding team, led by our flyweight star Jimmy Jackson. I got home from work at four o'clock that afternoon, revved up about the tournament—and there sat Charlotte with a packed bag and a pained expression on her face. She had been in labor for some time already, though somehow she had been able to prepare dinner for the kids. She needed to go to the hospital, right now. "We'd better get moving," she said. I called Phyllis Wheatley to tell my boxers what was happening and to ask that someone make sure the team got to the auditorium on time. We also called Charlotte's sister Margaret and arranged for her to come and stay with Rita and Butch. Then we raced to St.

Mary's Hospital with little time to spare. Ricky was born at 6:45 p.m. As soon as the doctor told me everything was well, I shot out of the hospital and headed to the Minneapolis Auditorium.

When I pulled up in front of the auditorium, it seemed everyone in the place had heard that I was absent because Charlotte was having a baby. The fellow out in front who directed us where to park knew the news when I pulled up, at about 7:15 p.m. He said, "You leave it there, Harry. Jimmy Jackson is getting ready to go in the ring and he's been hollering for you. I'll park your car." I ran into the auditorium, and they were just getting ready to announce Jimmy's match. When Jimmy saw me run in, boy, he was really pleased to see me. What a night I had! Word of the birth even made it into the *Star* and *Tribune* sports pages the next day. The paper said I came to the auditorium "with a smile broader than he sports when one of his fighters wins."

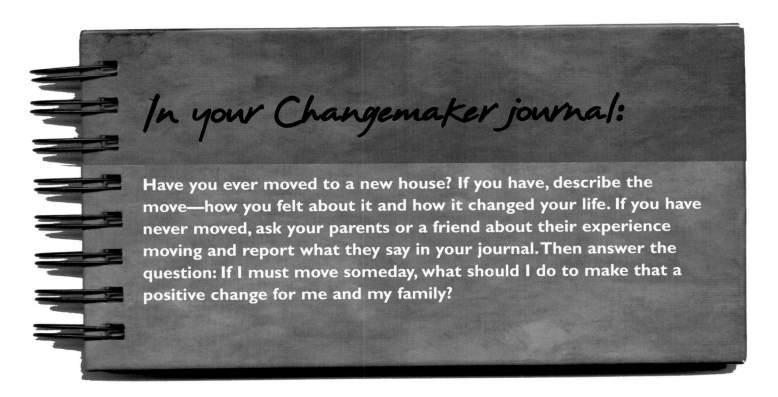

In your Changemaker journal:

Have you ever moved to a new house? If you have, describe the move—how you felt about it and how it changed your life. If you have never moved, ask your parents or a friend about their experience moving and report what they say in your journal. Then answer the question: If I must move someday, what should I do to make that a positive change for me and my family?

Border

AFTER OUR MARRIAGE, Charlotte and I were undecided about which church we would attend. Charlotte grew up at Border Methodist Church. I had gone to Wayman African Methodist Episcopal Church as a child. I also often attended Zion Baptist, the church near my sister's house. It was Rita's birth that settled the matter. Children should go to church with their mother, I reasoned. Rita was baptized at Border. I joined too. It proved to be a fateful choice.

Border had been founded in 1918. Its first building stood along the back of what is today the Minneapolis Farmers Market, on Border Avenue, which explains its name. By the time I joined, the church had been forced by development to move to a tiny stucco building at Fourth and Aldrich Avenues, a few blocks away.

When I joined, Border was a small congregation of about 150 members, many of them senior citizens. Along with Zion and Wayman, Border was a church that tried to combat racial injustice, poverty, and crime. Despite its small size, it had a good choir, a Sunday school for children, and active women's and men's clubs.

The Reverend Damon Young, the pastor of Charlotte's youth, spread Border's good name outside the neighborhood. Reverend Young was more than a pastor. He was a neighborhood leader, active at Phyllis Wheatley, in the NAACP, in city politics. He may have been the first Border pastor to get the attention of the city leaders who worshipped at Hennepin Avenue Methodist, the cathedral-style church about a mile away.

In race, income, worship style, and status, it is hard to imagine two congregations more opposite than Border and Hennepin. Yet the congregations had a connection. Some of the women who were leaders at Hennepin were also board members at Phyllis Wheatley. They became acquainted with Reverend Young and appreciated his work to keep young people away from crime in our neighborhood. A lot of other ministers in our neighborhood had second jobs; several were barbers and used their barbershops as church offices. But Reverend Young was trying to be a full-time minister and needed extra financial support to do so. Hennepin Church chipped in, and did so again when Border needed to relocate to Fourth and Aldrich in 1937 and build a parsonage.

To my regret, Damon Young left Border in the early 1940s. He went on to serve churches in Cincinnati, Detroit, and Chicago. In typical Methodist fashion, Border went through a string of pastors during the rest of that decade. In 1949, one came to stay: the Reverend Charles Sexton, a bright man from Jamaica. Born in 1894, he had degrees from five colleges and had a career as a research chemist before becoming a minister. He was a wonderful speaker and a true student of the faith. I have no doubt that if he had become a minister at a time when the Methodist Church was more welcoming of African Americans, he would have been the pastor of a large congregation.

Under Reverend Sexton, the bond between Hennepin and Border grew stronger. Hennepin was a leading church in Minneapolis in the 1950s. Among its four thousand members were city leaders in business and government, people with the means and the desire to make a difference in their community. As the civil-rights movement came to life in the rest of the country, Hennepin members were among the people in Minneapolis who wanted to do their part to end racial segregation in their own city. In 1955, Hennepin was among the first churches in Minnesota to adopt a policy that all races were welcome as members.

Some Hennepin members wanted Border as their church's partner in advancing racial understanding. Members at Border and Hennepin came to know each other through choir performances at each other's churches and through the women's and men's groups that were popular in those years. Charlotte was active in the women's group; Reverend Sexton recruited me for Methodist Men. Before I knew it, I had an assignment to help Methodist Men's clubs at four other Minneapolis churches recruit new members and develop programs. One of those four churches was Hennepin. I was adding to the bond between Border and Hennepin churches.

The two churches' connection was put to the test in 1955, when Border got word that its building was again in the path of a wrecking ball. Glenwood-Lyndale, the second big housing project to alter the shape of my neighborhood, was coming. (The first was Sumner Field, a segregated project near the park of the same name.) The plan was to tear down existing structures from Lyndale to Emerson Avenue, between Glenwood Avenue and Olson Highway—hence the name Glenwood-Lyndale. Sumner School's building, no longer in use as a school, would go. So would Border Church. A lot of the neighborhood's nicer homes were also slated for destruction. The Glenwood-Lyndale project would destroy much of the neighborhood's history.

Border's initial reaction was to fight the city's plan to tear down its building. But the congregation began to weaken when the city offered Border free land for construction of a new church and parsonage. That was an option worth considering, and we looked at it seriously. We asked hard questions about the congregation's future. Our church was down to about eighty-five members, most of them older people. If we were to build, should we build a tiny church to accommodate the members we had then, or should we build a bigger place and expect to grow? Would we be wise to go into debt for a big new church? Who would pay off a big mortgage?

By 1955, I had become Border's lay leader—the top administrative job a nonordained person can have in a Methodist congregation. That put me in the middle of the decision-making about the church's future. I was also in contact with my friends at Hennepin Church. Among them were Miriam Bennett, the wife of businessman Russell Bennett and a dedicated community volunteer, and Les Parks, the head of Baker Properties in downtown Minneapolis. They took an interest in Border's problem. "What's going to happen if Border chooses not to build a new church?" they asked me. I told them about our options, including the one that I feared was becoming most likely: we could dissolve the congregation, and members could scatter to other churches.

I did not like that prospect. It would mean losing contact with people who had become close friends. But as lay leader, I had to be practical. I had to consider the young families who would bear the financial burden of whatever decision we made. At a congregational meeting, I said, "I don't think we can rebuild unless we can greatly increase our membership in a very short time. If you vote tonight to build a new church, we'll go ahead and try to do it. But it's going to cause a burden on the next generation. They may not be able to handle it."

The motion to build a new church failed, and the Border congregation faced up to the likelihood that we would disband. As lay leader, I was still searching for a better alternative. I said as much to Miriam Bennett. Her response surprised me. She said, "Why don't we invite all of you to come to Hennepin?"

I could not believe at first that she meant what she had said. Despite the relationship that had been built between Hennepin and Border, it was still a giant leap to think that we could be one congregation. In the 1950s, race was a rigid dividing line on Sunday morning in America. Black and white people simply did not worship together. But Miriam Bennett was serious—one might say she was inspired. She took her idea back to Hennepin, and sold it with a determination that made her a wonder to behold. Timing was in her favor. The year was 1956. Only a few months earlier, a bus boycott by the black churches in Montgomery, Alabama, led by the young Reverend Martin Luther King Jr., had captured the nation's attention. Hennepin was one of many churches that admired King's efforts. Hennepin put a slogan on its front-lawn sign on Lyndale Avenue: "Welcome to people of all races." Miriam Bennett asked as she proposed a merger with Border, "Do we mean what we say on our sign?"

We had some selling to do at Border too. I liked her idea. I kept thinking about how good it would be to raise my children in a large church with a strong youth program. I shared those views with others at Border. I also spoke about the fine people I had met at Hennepin and my confidence in their goodwill. Mrs. Bennett, Les Parks, and another Hennepin layperson, Orem Robbins, came to a congregational meeting to help me convince Border members that Hennepin wanted to help Border.

We ended that meeting with a show-of-hands vote. Most of those present indicated that they were willing to join Hennepin. That put the weight back on Mrs. Bennett's shoulders to open Hennepin's doors to us. She did not have much trouble. Hennepin's lay leaders were behind the idea, and at Methodist churches, lay people usually make the governing decisions. I later heard that Mrs. Bennett had a little quiet lobbying help from a former teacher at Hennepin's University of Life program for young adults, U.S. Senator Hubert Humphrey. He placed a few calls to his Hennepin friends to let them know he supported what Mrs. Bennett was proposing.

The invitation from Hennepin for merger came in early December 1956. Border voted December 23 to accept. The merger was warmly received but not unanimously accepted. A few Border members who did not feel comfortable worshipping in a large, mostly white congregation scattered to other churches. Perhaps four or five families left Hennepin in protest. The Minnesota Methodist Conference bishop, D. Stanley Coors, took some abuse for his enthusiastic support. He received threatening hate mail, promising revenge by the Ku Klux Klan. Nevertheless, the merger went forward with no visible protest or disruption.

Border Church's Hattie Dryer Circle hosted an annual George Washington tea, often attended by women from Hennepin Avenue Methodist Church. In line facing the camera are Charlotte, her sister Margaret NaPue, and Ruth Majors.

On January 6, 1957, the first joint worship service between Hennepin and Border was conducted. Two weeks later, on January 20, sixty-seven Border Methodists transferred their membership to Hennepin Church. It was an emotional time for both congregations. None of us knew then quite how important the day was. We later learned that ours was only the second merger of a white and a black Protestant congregation in the United States.

Reverend Sexton did not join us at Hennepin. He went on to make some history of his own. For about eight months after the merger, he was a substitute minister in a number of places, including the Champlin Methodist Church near Anoka, a tiny, all-white parish in the country. In September 1957, little Champlin voted to call Reverend Sexton as its permanent pastor. Champlin became the first all-white congregation in the nine-state Methodist jurisdiction to be served by a black pastor.

The Border merger has become a source of pride for Hennepin. Hennepin's chapel was renamed Border Chapel in 1994. Many former Border members are still Hennepin members, as are our children and grandchildren. Other people of color have joined in the intervening years. We are no longer pioneers, but full participants in a church that has become fully our own.

In your Changemaker journal:

Harry Davis's friends at Hennepin Church helped him make changes that solved a problem. Describe a time when you helped a friend solve a problem or when a friend helped you. What kind of relationship did you have that allowed one of you to be helpful to the other? What are the qualities of a friendship that can encourage positive change?

Stirring 11

NO AFRICAN AMERICAN in the 1950s was spared the sting of racism. No one was unaware of the efforts being made by brave people, both black and white, to overcome it. Busy as I was in those years, the stirring of the civil-rights movement touched me. I followed the news of federal troops forcing an all-white high school in Little Rock, Arkansas, to admit black students, and of African Americans refusing to ride city buses in Montgomery, Alabama, because of the back-of-the-bus seating rule for people of color.

I looked for a chance to get more involved in the organization that had been the champion of racial equality all my life: the National Association for the Advancement of Colored People, or the NAACP. My chance came with my change in duties in the Golden Gloves program in 1960. My years of spending five nights per week in a gymnasium ended. A greater cause was about to fill my calendar.

The NAACP was founded in 1909 in New York and came to Minneapolis in 1914, a year after an NAACP chapter was founded in St. Paul. But the organization was weak until it became linked with Phyllis Wheatley Settlement House and Gertrude Brown. Miss Brown made the NAACP her partner in lifting the sights of people of color, particularly young people. The Junior NAACP, a teenagers' group, was combined with the Wheatley's activities for young people. In NAACP classes we learned the basics about politics. We learned about the precinct, the ward, the district, and the caucus. We learned parliamentary procedure, party organization, and voter registration. In election years, we went door-to-door with the organization's senior members, registering voters and distributing literature for candidates we supported. We went out again on election day to get out the vote. The message that was drilled into us, over and over, was the importance of the vote.

I was a young coach at Phyllis Wheatley after World War II, when returning GIs and idealistic young people got behind a new mayor, Hubert Humphrey, to begin a civil-rights movement in Minneapolis. I came to know many of the leaders in that cause, thanks to my Junior NAACP teacher, Cecil Newman.

Cecil Newman taught practical politics to more than a generation of young African Americans in Minneapolis. He was the publisher and editor of the *Minneapolis Spokesman* and *St. Paul Recorder,* newspapers he founded in 1934 to serve the black community. He was a voice for black people within the Democratic-Farmer-Labor Party. He was forever writing editorials and speaking out, criticizing the unfair treatment of black people in Minneapolis hotels and restaurants and in housing and employment. He complained when well-trained black attorneys were denied admission to the bar and when black doctors were not allowed to practice in some hospitals. He told me and my friends at Phyllis Wheatley that our generation of black Americans had greater potential than any generation before it to change all of that, especially if we educated ourselves about politics. Politics could be the means of getting out of the hole, he said.

When I first met Cecil, I wasn't sure I liked him. He was so serious, strict, and strong-minded. He expected a lot of the students in his classes. But as I got to know him, I discovered that he was patient, caring, and considerate. He modeled the kind of life he wanted us to live—disciplined and devoted to high purpose. Cecil would never back off on any issue. The more I listened to him, the more I thought, "Here's a guy I want to learn from."

Cecil made a point of introducing me to Humphrey in the spring of 1945, during the final weeks of Humphrey's campaign for mayor. He was the featured speaker at the NAACP annual banquet at Phyllis Wheatley. It was a huge formal affair. As the Wheatley boxing coach, I was one of the serving crew. We flipped a coin and I won the right to serve the head table. The head table was by the exit door on the west side of the room. The food would come up in dumbwaiters, or small elevators, on the northeast side, so the waiter for the head table always got a workout, carefully carrying large trays of food across the room. Cecil was seated next to Humphrey, and as I worked, I became aware that they were watching me and appeared to be talking about me. When I got close to them and began to serve Cecil, he said to Humphrey, "This is the former president of our junior chapter, Harry Davis. I'm sure that someday he will be president of the senior chapter. He's our boxing coach here. I'm sure you have read about him in the paper, about the Golden Gloves."

Humphrey stood to greet me. "Yes, I have. Yes, I have," he said, pumping my hand. "You do very well, young man. You know how to treat people. You keep that up and someday you may be mayor of Minneapolis." I walked away thinking, "What a dreamer." But I never forgot his words. They raised my sights.

When Humphrey became mayor, he did not disappoint his NAACP allies. He insisted that the police crack down on the criminals who ran illegal gambling and prostitution rings in my neighborhood. He cleaned house at police headquarters, demoting or firing cops who were shielding gangsters from justice. He insisted that all parts of the city receive police protection. He ordered hotels and restaurants to serve people of color, and backed up that order with a threat that their city licenses to operate would be in jeopardy if they did not comply. Further, he directed the police to enforce his order. He told black citizens, "If you go into a restaurant and you are refused a seat when you see plenty of empty tables, go outside and get a police officer. Be sure to take the badge number of the police officer," he added, knowing that cops on the beat might need a nudge to play their part. Humphrey also leaned hard on the University of Minnesota to integrate its student housing. He announced that he believed that any student who came to the public university had a right to be housed in campus housing. Just like that, the university fell into line. He made the same point to the private colleges in Minneapolis and St. Paul, and they too integrated their dormitories. It was the end of college students living at Phyllis Wheatley. Humphrey quickly got a reputation as a politician who promised a lot and then kept his promises. When he ran for reelection in 1947 and for the U.S. Senate in 1948, I was among his volunteers, distributing literature and urging people to vote for Humphrey.

I remained a member of the NAACP during the 1950s, even though I was not able to be very active. I liked to think that I was doing my part when I urged my boxers to be aware of events in their communities, and, when they were old enough, to vote.

It was in the 1950s at an NAACP state meeting that I first heard the Reverend Dr. Martin Luther King Jr. speak, soon after he led the famous bus boycott in Montgomery, Alabama. He was a very young man but self-assured and in command of any crowd. What a preacher he was! The meeting that day turned into a preaching contest of sorts, with each speaker trying to outdo the others. After Dr. King spoke, an audience was ready to get out and march and do things. He wasn't a big man, he wasn't imposing, but he had such confidence. I heard him speak several more times, but I never had the privilege to know him personally.

I became more active in the NAACP just as the civil-rights movement was picking up steam nationally. The national NAACP was working to get more black people to vote, especially in the South, where unfair election laws had been keeping them away from the polls for more than seventy-five years. NAACP chapters in northern states like Minnesota were asked to recruit new members and raise money for that work. I headed the ambitious 1964 chapter-membership drive. Our goal was to add one thousand names to our existing roster of fifteen hundred members. I set up a membership campaign team that eventually grew to 320 people. We had to extend the drive a month past its original deadline, but we made our goal.

Soon after that success, I was elected president of the Minneapolis NAACP chapter. My opponent in that election was the Reverend Stanley King of Sabathani Baptist Church, a critic of our NAACP chapter's approach to civil rights. We had always stressed education as the best way to end racial injustice. That was too slow for Stan and his followers. They wanted the Minneapolis chapter to demand full equality between the races *right now.* The chapter's old guard saw Stan as a troublemaker. I was the old guard's choice, but I tried to be a bridge between the two camps. I wasn't opposed to peaceful protest. I had seen the power of demonstration twenty-five years earlier when Marian Anderson was denied admission to Minneapolis's Dyckman Hotel. But I believed there were many alternatives to protest that might produce better results in the long run.

After becoming chapter president, I found myself wearing the label "civil rights leader" and being asked by local reporters for comments about civil-rights news around the country. For example, I was called upon for comments in August 1965 after several days of some of the worst race riots the nation had ever witnessed, in the Watts neighborhood of Los Angeles. I saw the destruction there as a setback for civil rights. "We've come so far now that a Los Angeles (riot) won't stop us," I said. "But it is unfortunate, because the rioters are destroying the very thing we as a people have been fighting for—the right to live in freedom and peace without fear of violence or the destruction of property." I also said that we would never see such a thing in Minneapolis. I prayed that I was right.

But Minneapolis was no longer quiet or small. It was growing and becoming more like other big cities in the country. The racial anger that bubbled up in places like Los Angeles and Detroit was present in Minneapolis too.

Early on the morning of August 3, 1966, about fifty young black people walking on Plymouth Avenue, returning from a late-night picnic, began pelting pebbles and stones at cars carrying white people. Things escalated, as they often do when young people are together and a little drunk. The kids went into Silver's Food Market at 1711 Plymouth, and when they were asked to leave, they filled their pockets and overturned display shelves on their way out. Then rocks were thrown at other store windows along Plymouth Avenue. The kids helped themselves to cigarettes from Hy's Dairy Deli, broke windows at Gold's Clothing, and stole hunting knives and made a mess at Plymouth Hardware. Koval's Furniture and Appliance probably got the worst of it; about thirty portable television sets were stolen.

I was one of about fifty people who got word of the disturbance with a call at daybreak from Mayor Arthur Naftalin's office, summoning me to a meeting at 10:00 a.m. at City Hall to decide what should be done in response. I was surprised to see Governor Karl Rolvaag present when I arrived. Several business leaders were there too.

I told the mayor that he should focus on the root of

the problem: idleness and poverty among black teenagers, caused by a refusal of white employers to hire them. Stan King, my NAACP rival, was there too. He offered to arrange a quiet meeting in a park between the mayor, the governor, and some of the kids who had done the damage the night before. To Mayor Naftalin's credit, he accepted Stan's offer and agreed that there would be no police present and that none of the kids would be arrested. The purpose would be to hear the kids out. I was at the meeting a few days later, at Oak Park. We sat on benches and talked. The kids said, "What we want is jobs *now*. And we don't want people, when we get hired, to harass us on the job." Mayor Naftalin told them that he would see what could be done.

The next day, I was again at a meeting at the mayor's office. He had a clever idea. He would open the hallway outside his office in City Hall for a job fair. Several business leaders said they could make a few dozen jobs available on short notice and would be glad to send their personnel officers to City Hall to receive applications. Young people could come and apply for jobs without being subject to arrest as they did. The number of jobs available was small, but it was a start. Mayor Naftalin was criticized for trying so hard to satisfy lawbreakers. I thought he acted like a wise leader.

I was saddened that most of the stores that were damaged on Plymouth Avenue were owned by Jewish people. Jews and blacks had lived together as friends in my old neighborhood for more than half a century, but events of the 1950s and 1960s were pulling them apart. Most of our Jewish neighbors had moved out in the 1950s, when other parts of the city began to welcome them as homeowners. They continued to own stores on the North Side. It did not take long for frustrated young black people to begin to think of them not as neighbors, but as white folks who lived in comfort someplace else. The shops became a near-at-hand symbol of what white people had and black people did not.

I wanted the NAACP to try to bring blacks and Jews in Minneapolis back together. I called a community meeting two weeks later at a North Side church, billing it as a speak-out session on race relations in our city. When my turn to speak came, I said, "We do not condone the vandalism by Negro youths against the Jewish merchants on Plymouth Avenue. There is no anti-Jewish feeling in the NAACP, and we hope there is no anti-Negro sentiment in the Jewish community now. Our Jewish neighbors have been our oldest allies in the struggle for civil rights. They remain our partners in that struggle." I hoped I was right.

That tense summer ended, and an uneasy truce settled over the North Side. When summer returned, the truce held—until the night after the 1967 Aquatennial Torchlight Parade in downtown Minneapolis. A black man, Samuel Simmons, was shot at Wayne's Bar shortly before midnight, allegedly by the bar's white owner. It was all the spark that was needed. At 2:00 a.m., I was roused from a sound sleep by the telephone. It was Mayor Naftalin, who said, "Harry, I'm up here with the riot squad on Plymouth and Humboldt." I knew the corner; a vacant lot was there. "Almost all of the stores on Plymouth Avenue are burning," he said. "They're on fire." He paused for a moment for me to take in this bad news, then he said, "I would appreciate it if you could come up here right away. I've called some other people too. I'm hoping we can prevent a full-scale riot."

I quickly got dressed and drove as fast as I dared to find the mayor. I was upset by what Naftalin told me but not shocked. I had been worried for weeks about the possibility that one nasty episode would be enough to trigger more violence. But I was not prepared for the sight of Plymouth Avenue shops burning from Penn Avenue all the way to Humboldt, eight blocks away. There was no fighting. There was no gunfire. There was only fire—fire everywhere, it seemed—and scared, agitated people milling about. It was a case of massive arson—and an act of great stupidity too. How could people be so foolish as to make a point by destroying their own neighborhood? Would they burn down their own houses to impress someone? Only three grocery stores still operated on all of Plymouth Avenue that summer. Early on July 20, all three were destroyed. For decades afterward, North Side residents would complain that their neighborhood did not have enough grocery stores. It made no sense.

The scene that night was nightmarish. The stench of smoke was oppressive, the heat intense enough to break display windows. Streets were blocked. Mayor Naftalin had given my name and car license number to the police, and told them to let me pass the barricade. He had done the same for several other black leaders he had summoned. There sat the riot squad, fifty or sixty officers strong, with a cluster of squad cars, lights flashing. Police captains were standing by, waiting for orders from Chief of Police Cal Hawkinson. He was sitting in the mayor's car. I was directed to join them there.

Mayor Naftalin and Chief Hawkinson were discussing whether to send the riot squad down the street with orders to arrest everyone. I urged the mayor and police chief not to do that. "There are too many people on the street, and too many of them are women and children," I argued. "They live here. They are in the street because their homes are in danger. That isn't a reason to arrest people." Further, we said, a sweep of the streets this long after the fires started was not likely to catch the culprits. The people who set the fires weren't going to stick around after the blaze got going. Arrests then would only risk injuring innocent people, and if that happened, we argued, the police might have a real riot on their hands. "If people see kids getting hit, they're going to respond," I said.

The mayor quickly saw our point. "Yes, we can't put our citizens' lives in danger," he said. "The people in the street don't know who started the fires." He refused to order the riot squad to move. That decision disappointed some of the officers on the street, including the head of the Police Federation, a lieutenant named Charlie Stenvig.

Mayor Naftalin decided that the riot squad would clear the street only if the crowd interfered with firefighting. It did not. When fire engines arrived, people backed away and gave them room to work. That convinced Mayor Naftalin and Chief Hawkinson that the people on the street were not rioters. We then agreed that, after the fire engines did their jobs, we would approach people and ask them to go home. Only then, if they refused, would the police move in. Their orders would be to arrest only those who were caught stealing from the stores.

That was how we met the dawn that morning on Plymouth Avenue. There was plenty of destruction, but no one was hurt, very few people were arrested, and the streets were rather calm. We considered that a major achievement. Plymouth Avenue remained a hot spot for several more days. Early on July 21, there were episodes of rock throwing and fistfights and reports of gunshots. It was minor stuff compared with the night before. Nevertheless, Mayor Naftalin called Governor Harold LeVander and asked for help from the National Guard. Six hundred guards were on the scene the next evening, a Friday. A dance was held at The Way, a new youth center. Under the watchful eyes of parents and National Guard troops, the dance proceeded without trouble. What came to be called the "Plymouth Avenue riot" was over.

I always suspected that the mayor called the National Guard not out of concern about more violence, but to give Minneapolis police a break. Mayor Naftalin was smart, and he knew the city's police force well. It was not a happy group. Many cops, including Charlie Stenvig and his Police Federation friends, wanted to use more force against angry young black people. The mayor knew that too much contact between cops and black kids was not a good idea just then.

For months after the Plymouth Avenue riot, Mayor Naftalin and Chief Hawkinson were criticized for what some people said was their mild response to lawbreakers. It was a bad rap. I'm convinced that their restraint saved lives. I told the mayor that I thought he had done the right thing: "If that had been my son on the street, and one of the police officers had hurt him, I wouldn't just stand there and let that happen. Either I'm going to get hurt, or that police officer is going to get hurt. You acted in the interests of public safety."

That episode sealed my friendship with Art Naftalin. Along with Cecil Newman, Mayor Naftalin was my mentor in politics. He was a magnet, drawing people to him with his ideas and integrity. He was such an organizer. In August 1965, he tapped me for membership on the Fair Employment Practices Commission. In 1968 he had a new assignment for me: a seat on the city's Civil Service Commission. I was the first black person ever to serve on that three-member panel, which reviewed the rules and regulations governing city employment. The mayor's instructions to me were to find out why the city had hired no black police officers or firefighters and very few other black employees. "I understand that a lot of people are taking the examinations, but they aren't getting hired," he told me. "Find out why."

I looked into it, and found that the vast majority of the black applicants had passed the written examination, but failed the oral examination. That test was an interview before a panel of police or fire officials or city managers. I found that a particular mark had been drawn on the application forms of all the black applicants who had passed the written exam. All of the candidates whose forms bore that mark failed their oral exam. That mark, I concluded, was a signal to the people administering the oral exams that it was up to them to keep those applicants from being hired. I brought that evidence to the Civil Service Commission with a demand that the practice stop. No one admitted that I had guessed the system of discrimination. But after that, stray marks no longer appeared on application forms. From that time on, black applicants began to pass both the written and the oral exams.

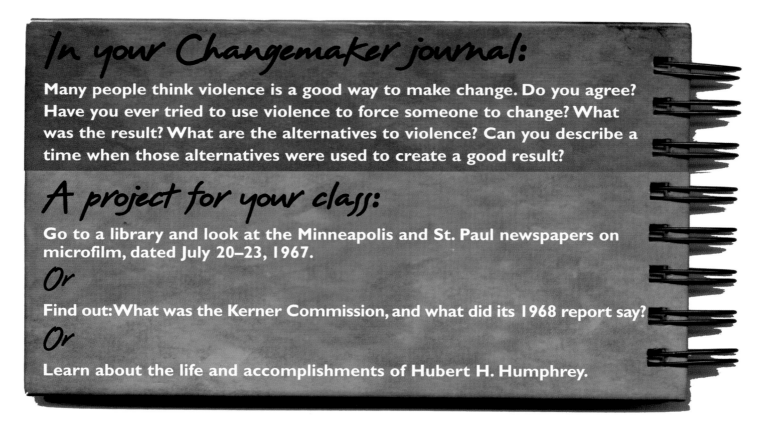

In your Changemaker journal:

Many people think violence is a good way to make change. Do you agree? Have you ever tried to use violence to force someone to change? What was the result? What are the alternatives to violence? Can you describe a time when those alternatives were used to create a good result?

A project for your class:

Go to a library and look at the Minneapolis and St. Paul newspapers on microfilm, dated July 20–23, 1967.

Or

Find out: What was the Kerner Commission, and what did its 1968 report say?

Or

Learn about the life and accomplishments of Hubert H. Humphrey.

Mobilizing 12

FOR PEOPLE OF COLOR—indeed, for all Americans—the late 1960s were a time when hope and despair, victories and losses, all collided in the span of a few intense years.

When Lyndon Johnson became president of the United States in 1963, he set out to improve the lives of poor Americans. His program was called the "War on Poverty." In 1966, the War on Poverty arrived in Minneapolis, with instructions to establish a board of citizens that would apply for, receive, and decide how to spend federal money on education, housing, and health care for the poor. Mayor Art Naftalin appointed me to the new board, called the Hennepin County Mobilization of Economic Resources Board, or MOER Board for short. If Minneapolis were to get its share of federal money, it would be up to the MOER Board to find it.

The new board was organized in August 1967. It was a strong group of sixty-six people, including leaders from business, government, and neighborhood organizations. Its first president was Elva Walker, a well-to-do community volunteer and a member of the family that founded the Walker Art Center. I was elected vice president of the board.

The first thing we tackled was an expansion of Head Start, the program for preschool children that started as a six-week summer program in 1966. It was our proudest accomplishment. We decided to make Head Start a joint project of the MOER Board and the Minneapolis School District. By 1968, Head Start was a year-round program, serving about one thousand four-year-olds. It's still going strong today.

We also immediately addressed the need for good-paying jobs for young people of color, particularly young parents. A lot of young fathers in the black community were unemployed or, more often, employed in jobs that paid low wages. They needed more education to secure a higher-wage job. We responded by creating the Twin Cities Opportunity Industrialization Center, or TCOIC, in 1967.

TCOIC quickly had more applications for training than it could handle. The program started by training young women for office jobs. Those first graduates had jobs waiting for them, courtesy of some of the business executives of the MOER Board. The CEO at Honeywell would offer to hire some number of the graduates, and soon the head of the Bemis Company was chiming in, matching the Honeywell offer. The executives' desire to top each other in hiring minority workers was just the opposite of the attitudes businesses had displayed only a few years earlier. TCOIC today has evolved into Summit Academy OIC, which sits in the heart of my old neighborhood, at 935 Olson Memorial Highway.

The MOER Board also got busy addressing health and housing problems. When I was young, we could go to Phyllis Wheatley to get vaccinations or treatment for colds and flu. That service was gone by the 1960s. The NAACP had been looking for a way to reestablish free or low-cost health services in the neighborhood. So the MOER Board applied to the federal Department of Health, Education, and Welfare for funds to establish a branch facility of Minneapolis General Hospital, the big downtown public hospital that was soon to change its name to Hennepin County Medical Center. We got the funds we asked for, and the result was the establishment of Pilot City Health Services on Penn Avenue. It still operates at the same site we chose, the old Beth El Synagogue.

We tackled the housing problem by forming neighborhood councils throughout the city and making low-interest loans for housing available through those groups. Our program was called Model Neighborhoods. Many city neighborhoods got their names through the Model Neighborhoods program.

The MOER Board was considered one of the most successful War on Poverty operations in the nation. Yet we were frustrated by a lot of government regulations, congressional budget cuts, and the controversy that swirled around our big, sixty-six-member board. It was a mostly white group trying to serve mostly black people, and that made some people in the black community mistrust us. They saw the ease with which Head Start and TCOIC were started, and they believed the War on Poverty could work all kinds of miracles just as quickly. They wanted more, and they wanted it now. A few of them wanted a personal share of the action. When that did not happen, they became unhappy.

At the first meeting of the full MOER board, on September 25, 1967, a group with complaints about the board's composition was so disruptive that Elva Walker stopped the meeting about halfway through the agenda. Matt Eubanks of the East Side Citizens Community Center was loudly complaining that the board did not adequately represent the city's poor neighborhoods. The problem was that the people chosen to represent the community were those who had become leaders of organizations such as the NAACP or the Urban League, and the poorest people often were not involved in organizations. I suspected that Matt's real goal was not representation. It was to get his hands on federal money.

Matt represented the more militant thinking that was coming to the fore among younger black people, in Minneapolis and around the country. They doubted that talking with politicians or filing lawsuits would ever produce justice for people of color. They put their faith in protests and violence instead. The Black Panthers organization sprang from that attitude. Division developed in the black community between the younger, impatient group and those who preferred to work for civil rights in the courts and through politics, such as the NAACP. I was plainly in the latter camp, so much so that more than once I was publicly called an Uncle Tom. That was the unkind name used for a black man who tried too hard to please white people. But I was connected through boxing with some of the younger people, and I tried to stay on good terms with them.

With Matt Eubanks, that was difficult. He did not believe in peaceful work. He was a native of Kansas City, Missouri, and had spent years studying at the University of Minnesota and traveling around the country to join civil-rights protests. He landed a job as a community organizer and attracted a following among young men who wanted to bring about change by force.

At that first MOER meeting, Matt and his young allies entered the room as if they were an invading military force. They were dressed in army camouflage clothing that looked like it had been worn for weeks. They circled the room until they had blocked every door and surrounded the audience. Then one of them yelled, "We want this meeting stopped. If you don't stop the meeting, we're going to stop the meeting." Then they pulled back their jackets to show that they were wearing guns on their sides. People squealed in fear. Matt's goal was to intimidate us—and he succeeded.

At our second meeting, Matt made another dramatic entrance and demanded more money for the Citizen Community Centers. Minneapolis had three of them. They were small storefront operations that made people aware of low-cost opportunities for housing money or job training, such as that offered at TCOIC. Matt argued that, on that basis, some TCOIC funds should flow to the little center on the East Side, where he was a staff member. "That can't be done," Elva Walker said. "We are not allowed to mix the money." They said, "If we don't get it, you don't get out these doors." It was like a holdup.

Elva had chaired many a meeting in her time, but she had never dealt with anything like this. As the vice chair, I was sitting next to her and tried to help her. I recognized some of the guys in Matt's group as kids from Phyllis Wheatley. I knew them well enough to feel confident that they had no intention of pulling those guns. "Let's just get through this meeting. Then we'll make sure that they don't come in with guns anymore," I whispered to her. So she told Matt's group that the board would make a special request of the federal agencies to see if the rules could be broken in this case. Then Elva excused herself to go to the bathroom and asked me to take her place as chair of the meeting. She didn't come back—ever. Suddenly, I was MOER Board chair.

When that meeting ended, I asked a few board members to discuss what had happened. I suggested that we meet the next morning at City Hall. "We've got tell the City Council that they need to pass an ordinance about carrying guns with live ammunition in holsters," I said. Carrying concealed weapons was against the law in Minneapolis then, but visibly carrying a loaded gun was not.

Never had I seen such quick response from city hall. Before the next day was over, the City Council had passed a ban on carrying a loaded gun without a permit. Two uniformed police officers were assigned to be present at all future MOER Board meetings. At our next meeting, when Matt came in with his gang, he made a point of showing that they were not carrying guns. They had a shouting match in mind. They said, "You made it illegal for us to carry weapons here. But we'll stop this meeting anyway. We don't want the cops in here." Some members of Matt's group were wearing holsters containing toy guns, just as a test of the new law. The police would not let them in. That produced a disturbance outside the meeting.

That was my first full meeting as chair. I was trying hard to keep order. Suddenly, in walked Dr. Herman B. Dilliard. He was a surgeon at the University of Minnesota, one of the first black men to hold that position. He was a large man, the largest brother from a family of big people—one of whom, his brother George, had come to the meeting with Matt. Herman weighed about 350 pounds, stood about six-foot-six, and had great big hands. I knew him well. He had been one of my boxers at Phyllis Wheatley. By 1967, he was "into the sixties." He sported a large Afro and often wore bib overalls. The effect was to make him seem about the size of a small house. He walked into our meeting carrying a carbine and two .45s with pearl handles. These were no toys. He looked at the police and said, "Which one of you SOBs will stop me?" The officers gave no response, other than to back away. He walked down the center aisle and sat in the front row, right in front of me. The meeting came to a halt, as everyone watched to see what would happen next.

Herman addressed me. "Harry, you're the chair?" I said, "Yes." He said, "I understand that there are some people walking in here with guns and threatening you guys." I tried to keep things cool. I said, "I think we've got it straightened out, Herman. Those fellows that are lined up around the back there came in, and we had a disagreement." He said, "I just want them to know that if anybody is here to interfere, if anybody threatens you . . ." He paused, stood, displayed his carbine, then flipped one of his pistols in his hand, gunslinger-style. You should have seen those cops look. You should have seen his brother and the rest of them. He announced to the room, "If any of you sons of bitches puts a hand on him," meaning me, "expect to see this." He stood and stared at them for a long moment, then he walked out. I remember thinking, "That Phyllis Wheatley coaching is sure paying off!"

I did not back away from Matt Eubanks. One day after we turned down another of his demands for money, he asked to meet privately with me at a store on Plymouth Avenue. I knew what was likely to happen there. He was planning another intimidation exercise, with no police or Herman Dilliard around to protect me. I agreed to the meeting, but I arranged for some intimidation of my own. I brought along two of my heavyweight Golden Gloves boxers. Matt hesitated to let me in when I showed up with my two companions. I said, "If they can't come in, I don't come in either." So we all sat down, and while we talked, Matt had some guys walk through the room and glare at us. Then the meeting ended and we left. Nothing was resolved, except perhaps Matt's ideas about how to get his way with the MOER chair.

Even though Matt and his thugs stopped carrying guns into our meetings, they continued to harass the board. We moved from small meeting halls, where they could easily surround us, to a big room in the Minneapolis Auditorium. We beefed up the police presence. I hated to ask people to come to a meeting that was supposed to be about community improvement under such conditions, but I couldn't ask volunteers to put themselves in harm's

way. It was a tough situation.

Matt seemed to thrive on creating stress for others. He had the entire University of Minnesota on edge in January 1969, when he persuaded a group of black students to occupy Morrill Hall, the administration building, to demand the creation of a black-studies program. Such a program was needed. A student could take just about any European language at the university, but no African languages. A student could learn about every aspect of European history and culture, but find very few courses about Africa's past or present. Contemporary black authors rarely appeared in course descriptions. I don't object to nonviolent protest, but I wasn't happy with Matt and his idea of occupying the administration building. He was putting young students right out front and possibly in harm's way. Who would be hurt if the university asked the governor to send the National Guard to clear the building? Not Matt.

Fortunately, the university president was Malcolm Moos, a wise, peace-loving man. The building takeover began the afternoon of January 14. That evening, President Moos called several African American MOER Board members to a meeting to discuss ways to end the siege at Morrill Hall without violence. One of those present was Oscar Howard, the owner of a restaurant and catering business. He was with us because we were at a meeting at his restaurant when President Moos tracked us down, and we invited him to come along. We made an agreement with President Moos: He would not ask the governor to send the National Guard for at least a few days, and we would go to Morrill Hall in small groups the next day and attempt to reason with the students and negotiate an end to the standoff.

I said I would make the first foray to Morrill Hall, and Oscar agreed to be my partner. We were allowed to enter and encountered Matt Eubanks coming out the door as we were coming in. He laughed when he saw me. He had been expecting me, he said, and had been telling the students that I was an Uncle Tom whom they could ignore. He was a terrific speaker, the kind who could get you to walk a tightrope, even if you were scared to death. I steeled myself for a big challenge. But the students seemed willing to listen to me, so I told them about my background, about my life in north Minneapolis, what I planned to do when I was a youngster, how I had been inspired by Cecil Newman and Gertrude Brown and others to live my life trying to make a difference. I told them about Hubert Humphrey and how he changed the housing practices at the university. I told them that I thought their complaint about the university had merit. "But the last thing in the world that I would do is encourage you to take over this place and fight an opponent that you are not equipped to fight," I said. "The police can come in here and beat you and kill you. You're disrupting a great university. You're doing damage to this building. You're destroying property, and maybe you'll even destroy someone's

life. You would be responsible for that. I would never put you in that position. I don't know who talked to you. Whatever they told you about making changes, you can't make them by trying to hurt somebody else."

By then it was about 9:00 a.m., and I saw no evidence that anyone had had any breakfast. I asked, "Are you hungry?" The kids said, "Yes, we haven't eaten since yesterday." It was a great thing that Oscar was there. I suggested that he call his catering service and bring the students some breakfast. He called, and in a short while, trucks loaded with food pulled up to Morrill Hall. We called President Moos, and he directed the university police to let the trucks pass. All the kids were fed. We had a very interesting conversation after that because the kids were full and they were willing to open up and do some serious negotiating. At about noon the students agreed to end their takeover, and President Moos announced that he was willing to take the first steps in creating a black-studies department. It was a good resolution.

Matt Eubanks's harassment of the MOER Board eventually came to the attention of the Office of Economic Opportunity in Chicago, our parent organization. He was turning his Citizens Community Center into a staging ground for demonstrations and protests, which was not allowed under the guidelines for receiving federal funds. OEO threatened to yank the money from all CCC programs in Minneapolis. More than $400,000 a year was on the line. I went to Chicago to negotiate a plan that would keep the money flowing. I knew that Matt had to resign to settle the matter, but I also knew that I would cause an uprising among his followers if I were to try to fire him. Matt finally figured out for himself that he had to go. But he did not go quietly. He fought the compromise I had reached that kept the Minneapolis CCCs funded. At one MOER meeting where Matt and I did some verbal sparring, one of his young followers tried to do some real sparring with me. Matt had to restrain the young man.

Minneapolis Star columnist Jim Klobuchar put his finger on the spot I found myself in with the MOER Board. Klobuchar said I was "a guy caught in the middle . . . who right now has the militants' distrust and the establishment's sympathy and doesn't want either." Much as I believed in what the MOER Board was trying to accomplish, I wanted to find another way.

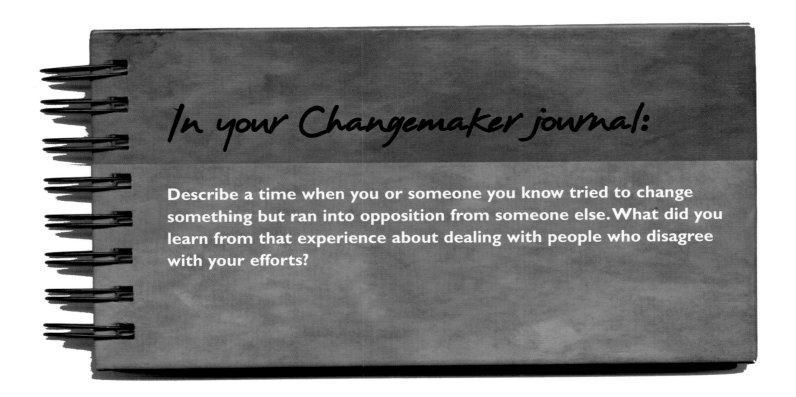

In your Changemaker journal:

Describe a time when you or someone you know tried to change something but ran into opposition from someone else. What did you learn from that experience about dealing with people who disagree with your efforts?

Coalescing 13

I RESIGNED FROM the MOER Board on February 1, 1970. I had found a way to be more effective in helping people of color. I had become executive director of the Minneapolis Urban Coalition.

Mayor Art Naftalin got Minneapolis involved in the nation's new Urban Coalition movement in August 1967. He was among a handful of big-city mayors who were determined to improve race relations in their cities. They wanted no more "long, hot summers" of tension and violence in black neighborhoods. They picked up on an idea of John W. Gardner, a member of President Lyndon Johnson's administration, for an organization that would bring government and business leaders together to change urban neighborhoods—hence the name Urban Coalition.

That August, Gardner called an "emergency" founding conference in Washington. Mayor Naftalin recruited forty Minneapolis business, government, and community leaders to attend. I was among them. It was another of the mayor's brilliantly organized plans. He persuaded members of that delegation to become the planning committee for the new Minneapolis Urban Coalition. He also put the arm on fourteen business leaders to contribute $1,000 apiece to get things started. By February 1968, the Minneapolis Urban Coalition was launched. Its leaders were businesspeople at the top of their corporations. Its plan was to apply the resources of the business community—money, talent, equipment, advice, community attention—to the needs of poor neighborhoods.

The young organization was less than two months old when it was put to a severe test. On April 4, 1968, the nation's leading voice for civil rights, the Reverend Dr. Martin Luther King Jr., was shot to death in Memphis, Tennessee. It was a devastating loss. I heard the news on the radio, having just come home for dinner after an Urban Coalition task-force meeting. I immediately turned on the television and heard a local newscaster saying, "It looks like there's going to be another riot in north Minneapolis. Young men are running up and down Olson

Highway." I jumped back into my car and headed to my old neighborhood. I knew that was where I needed to be.

I spotted a cluster of squad cars around Sumner Library and was not surprised to find Mayor Naftalin and several other Urban Coalition board members already there. The streets were full of upset, fearful people. I was a bit scared myself. When you wade into a crowd like that, you never know what is going to happen. But I was reassured to see no police decked out in riot gear and no sign of criminal activity.

We decided that the Urban Coalition should issue a public statement immediately. Fran Van Konynenburg from WCCO TV and Radio was there, and he offered to broadcast anything we wanted the community to hear. Some of us got busy writing. This is part of what our statement said: "Racism killed Dr. Martin Luther King. In recognition that such racism exists here in Minneapolis, though hopefully in less violent form, the Urban Coalition of Minneapolis will organize immediately an anti-racism program to deal in our area with this basic root of tragic violence in America."

The presence of the mayor and the squad cars attracted a good-sized crowd. We decided to use a police loudspeaker to address the people. A number of us took our turn with the loudspeaker, starting with the mayor. When it was my turn, I said, "Let's not make this look like Los Angeles or Detroit. Let's not tear up our own neighborhood. Dr. Martin Luther King was shot and killed. Our leader is lost, but this does not end our march for freedom."

Our message worked. People stayed in the street for a long time, but they were calm. After a public tragedy, people just want to be together, it seems. They want to hear someone saying something reassuring, like, "Martin Luther King is gone, but he would expect us to carry on. What we're doing here in Minneapolis is we're trying to get jobs, better housing, better education. We've got the Urban Coalition. We've got the MOER Board. We've got a chance to make things better." I said as much; so did other speakers. We also worked to correct rumors and keep tempers cool. One rumor was that white people were coming into the neighborhood to fight. Word spread that there was a car full of such people on Plymouth and Oliver Avenues. Some from our audience wanted to go and have it out with them. We said, "No, don't do that. We don't want a confrontation. Let the police do their job." It worked. There were riots in many American cities that night and over the next few days but not in Minneapolis.

It seemed that the murder of Dr. King spurred the young Urban Coalition to take decisive action in the months that followed. At a time when people desperately wanted to believe that America could be one country, the Urban Coalition was the new apostle of hope.

But in the first days after the assassination, it was the angry, impatient wing of the black community that came to us. A group that called itself a "steering committee of the black community" brought forward fourteen proposals for change in Minneapolis. They were presented as "demands," not recommendations, but the ideas were sound. I was asked to negotiate with the group on behalf of the Urban Coalition, and after only a few days the coalition responded with fourteen points of its own that embraced most of the steering committee's ideas. I called an all-city meeting at Phyllis Wheatley on April 15 and presented our points to the community. They became guideposts for action for the Urban Coalition in the years that followed. Among them: Better enforcement of laws against discrimination. Greater representation for minorities in

government, including more positions on the city's police and firefighting forces. Expansion of job training and hiring of minorities. A quick end to the war in Vietnam. Park and recreation improvements in black neighborhoods. Gun control. Elimination of racism in the judicial system. More college financial aid for minorities. More minority teachers in public schools, and better diversity training for all teachers. These were things the whole city could agree on. For days after we presented them to the community, my mailbox was full of letters from average citizens, expressing support and volunteering to help.

Still lacking as the weather warmed that spring was a full-time, permanent executive director for the Urban Coalition, a position that later was renamed president. I did not apply for the job. I thought I was busy enough. I was also, once again, a new father. Evan Wesley, our fourth child, was born January 16, 1968. He was a happy but rather surprising addition to our family, born more than twenty-four years after our eldest child, Rita. In fact, not long after Evan was born, Rita, who had married Joseph Lyell, announced that she was expecting her first child. Corey Lyell arrived fifteen months after Evan's birth. When Rita went back to her Northwestern National Bank career after maternity leave, Corey came to our house for day care. Charlotte had her hands full with babies once more. Corey and Evan were raised almost as brothers—and what a lively pair they were!

Ricky was in junior high when Evan was born, and

Mayor Art Naftalin and Fran Naftalin toasted Charlotte and me as we celebrated our twenty-fifth wedding anniversary in 1967. Charlotte was expecting our fourth child, Evan.

Butchie was in college at the University of Minnesota at Duluth. Both of them were very good athletes who kept us running to football games and track meets. Ricky kept our household lively in one other way. At Bryant Junior High School, he connected with a young musician named Roger Nelson. We had known Roger's mother, Mattie Del Shaw, and his aunt, Mattie's twin sister, Edna Mae, at Phyllis Wheatley. Roger started a rock band and Ricky played drums for him. They practiced in our basement until Charlotte said she could not stand the noise and moved them to the garage. Pretty soon our garage was the hangout of every kid in the neighborhood. Ricky eventually gave up the drums, but Roger Nelson stayed with his music and changed his name—to Prince.

With all that going on, I was not looking for a new job. But Mayor Naftalin called to say, "Harry, I've been talking with a lot of people—a lot of businesspeople and a lot of community people. We would all like to have you apply for the Urban Coalition job." He was persuasive, and I could not say no. A few days after I was interviewed for the job, I had a visit from Steve Keating of Honeywell and Dean McNeal of the Pillsbury Company. If I would take it, they said, the top staff job was mine.

Take it I did, and gladly, in July 1968. My arrangement was a leave of absence from Onan to last no longer than five years. The Onans were very accommodating. I think they were proud that a kid they had hired for one of the rock-bottom jobs in their plant had come so far.

Corey and Evan visit Santa Claus in 1973.

It did not take me long to decide that I wanted the Urban Coalition to be the focus of my work for my city. All the things that got in the way at the MOER Board— the federal rules, the sniping from people like Matt Eubanks—were not a problem for an organization run by business leaders. The Urban Coalition was going to have what it took to get action: money, talent, and, most important, power. The Urban Coalition had top people from its member corporations on its board. That meant that when a board member said that a loaned executive could be provided, or a certain number of job trainees could be employed, or a sum of money could be donated, they were speaking for their companies. When they said that government help was needed, they were saying that they would personally place a call to the governor or the senator. The power was sitting right there.

When corporate executives sat down for the first time to confront the needs of some of the poorest people in the city, real change began to happen. For example, when the Urban Coalition's law and justice task force heard complaints about police harassing black people and prosecutors treating them unfairly in the courts, the leading lawyers in town were there to hear them. They could assign junior lawyers at their firms to research complaints. They could talk with the judges. They knew the court system and could recommend ways to improve it. That task force changed the way the justice system responds to the black community.

It also made a big difference that Fran Van Konynenburg of WCCO was on our jobs task force. The black community wanted more minority people working for TV and radio stations. In those years, all the broadcasting reporters, editors, and producers were white. We thought that if black people had their share of those jobs, news coverage would more fully and accurately reflect the black experience. Fran picked up on that idea and contacted his fellow executives at the other three local television stations. They created what was called the Broadcasters' Skills Bank. It sought minority applicants for broadcast news jobs and steered them into the proper training. If applicants successfully completed the training, they had good assurance of a job. Soon the race barrier in local television journalism was broken.

Our education task force was important. John B. Davis, the supersmart superintendent of Minneapolis Public Schools, was on it. We recruited the head of the teachers federation and the principals organization as well.

We arranged for businesses to "adopt" schools in poorer neighborhoods and to bring more money, tutors, and mentors to those schools. That's what can happen when CEOs and the school superintendent sit around the same meeting table.

There was a positive reaction to the Urban Coalition. Still, the whole city was jittery about what would happen during the summer of 1968. It was an agonizing time for the whole nation. Robert Kennedy was killed in June; Hubert Humphrey's nomination for president was spoiled by police brutality in the streets of Chicago; and anger and despair over the loss of Martin Luther King darkened the outlook of black Americans.

That summer, as young people gathered at the city's lakes for relief from the heat, there were several near disasters. If a group of black youths arrived at Lake Calhoun and stood together in the parking lot or on the beach, some busybody would call the police and say that black kids were getting ready to start a riot. That would trigger a message to Mayor Naftalin, to the chief of police, and to me. I was the head of the Citizens Patrol Corps, the volunteer neighborhood watchdogs we assembled after the King assassination.

I was called the hot evening of July 9 at about 9:00 and told there was trouble across the street from Calhoun Beach Club. The police chief wanted my help. I drove there quickly and found a dangerous situation. About twenty members of the riot squad had assembled on one end of the beach. On the other side were about two dozen black teenagers and young adults. They were casting noisy remarks back and forth, but I saw no evidence that the kids had been doing anything wrong. Luckily, I had arrived before either side began advancing on the other. I sought out the officer in charge of the riot squad and asked for time to speak to the crowd. "Now, let's not create a riot," I said to him. "If you advance, these youngsters are not going to run. They are going to stand and fight. You're going to hurt them, and some of you are going to get hurt too. If you don't want your people hurt, let's try to talk this thing out." So we talked and talked, back and forth. The two sides stayed apart. I stood right in front of the kids. They were still taunting the cops, but I had the impression they weren't itching for a fight. I asked the kids to pipe down and stay calm. Meanwhile, a group of onlookers was assembling. Suddenly from the crowd, a Coke bottle came flying right into the middle of the police cluster. It landed hard on the shoulder of one of the officers. The reaction was quick. The police started moving toward the kids—and me. I thought, here I am, foolishly standing right in the line of fire. I yelled for them to stop. Somewhat to my surprise, as the police got near me, they did just that—and when they halted, so did the kids. Just about then, my friend Gleason Glover from the Urban League arrived and helped me disperse both crowds.

Moments like those jarred the city's peace of mind. But there was no race riot in Minneapolis in 1968, nor has

there been one since. For that, I think great credit is due the Urban Coalition. We made positive changes. The work of all of our task forces fit together. For example, the first house we bought in our scattered-site housing program—a big, run-down three-bedroom crate on Irving Avenue near Plymouth—was remodeled by a black

I met the founder of the National Urban Coalition, John W. Gardner, at a meeting in Washington while I headed the Urban Coalition in Minneapolis.

subcontractor from the neighborhood. We sold it to a family from the neighborhood with four children. Their father had been unemployed a short time before, but he had gone to TCOIC for training and landed a job made

Governor Wendell Anderson (second from left) and Mayor Charles Stenvig (fifth from left) were on hand in 1971 as we cut the ribbon opening First Plymouth Bank, the first bank on the near North Side.

available through the Urban Coalition. He got a home mortgage through the new bank the Urban Coalition launched. We referred him to places where he could get low-cost furnishings. We ushered that family from joblessness to home ownership, improved the neighborhood, and added to our city's security to boot.

That new bank, First Plymouth Bank, created a turning point in my life that I could not have predicted. I was one of its founding trustees. The bank's first president was John Warder, who owned a printing company, held a degree in finance, and was serving a term on the Minneapolis School Board. He decided when he took the bank job that he no longer had time for the school board and resigned. It was a decision that opened a new chapter in my life.

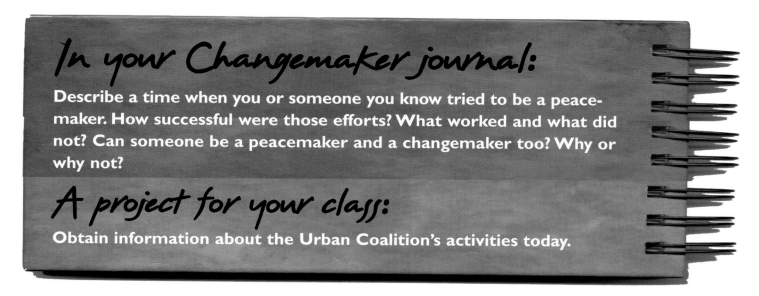

In your Changemaker journal:

Describe a time when you or someone you know tried to be a peacemaker. How successful were those efforts? What worked and what did not? Can someone be a peacemaker and a changemaker too? Why or why not?

A project for your class:

Obtain information about the Urban Coalition's activities today.

Desegregating 14

SCHOOL OFFICIALS WANTED to find another black person to take the open seat on the Minneapolis school board that had belonged to John Warder. The matter came up at one of the Urban Coalition executive committee's weekly breakfast meetings. I learned that certain business leaders had already talked with school-board members and Superintendent John B. Davis. They already had in mind a replacement, someone whom they said would be respected by school, business, and government leaders in the city. That someone was me.

I was flattered, but I was also aware of my already jam-packed calendar. I asked the business leaders to promise to give me more staff help for my work at the Urban Coalition and the MOER Board. When they agreed, I accepted an appointment to the vacant school-board seat. I was sworn in March 11, 1969. My term would expire in a little more than three months. If I wanted to keep the seat—and I did—I needed to run for election and start campaigning right away.

It was a big undertaking, but I felt prepared for it. I had been connected with Minneapolis Public Schools for almost my entire life. For a time, we had children in three different public schools, which meant Charlotte and I were active in three Parent-Teacher Associations (PTAs). One of them was at Central High School, the site of race-related protests in those years. That was in part because Central High School shared a building with Minneapolis Community College, attended by older, more politically aware students. The building was wide open to anyone who wanted to come in and stir things up. We PTA parents became concerned about our children's safety. The fire code required that school doors be open both ways all day. As a result, protesters were free to come in, walk the halls, and disrupt classes. When this was happening often, we recruited a group of PTA members to patrol the school corridors. We then appealed to the fire chief: "We want to be able to lock the doors from the inside. We have a group of parents who will be walking the halls. If

John B. Davis and I became good friends while he served as superintendent of schools in Minneapolis. We celebrated his eightieth birthday in 2001.

there is ever any fire or any trouble, we'll have people there to open the doors." The fire chief allowed us to try a lock-in at Central. It worked; the disruption of classes by protesters stopped. Parents in the neighborhood got to know each other better as a result. Those parents became a core group of support for my first school-board campaign.

The NAACP was my training ground for school politics. It was the nation's leading force for ending school segregation. It financed lawsuits that produced court decisions that prodded change. The Minneapolis School Board did not resist the NAACP's efforts, but neither did the board invite them. In those years, most school-board members came right out of the Minneapolis Club. They were well-motivated upper-class people, but they did not represent the community they served.

When John B. Davis became superintendent in 1967, he started pushing to hire more black people in school jobs, from janitor to assistant superintendent. He found promising young black teachers and groomed them as principals.

In one sense, Minneapolis schools had always been integrated: all students, black and white, attended the schools nearest their homes. But because the neighborhoods had been divided by color for decades, too many schools were all white. When I was a kid, people of color could live in only about a third of the city, and in most of those places they could only rent housing, not buy homes. They weren't allowed to buy houses or rent apartments elsewhere. That kind of discrimination was outlawed in the 1960s, but the established housing patterns continued. Superintendent Davis knew that if the right kind of lawsuit were brought, Minneapolis schools would likely face a court order to do something about segregation. He began talking about how to integrate Minneapolis schools.

His idea was to give all families, regardless of color, more school choices. Schools would offer different styles of teaching—Montessori, open, contemporary, continuous progress, fundamental. Families would have several schools from which to choose. As families made their choices, racial mixing would naturally occur, he believed.

Superintendent Davis got money from the federal government in 1969 to give his idea a try in the southeast part of the city. The Southeast Alternative Program was the result. Although parents weren't promised that their children would be admitted to their first-choice program, most were, and virtually every family was accepted at either their first or second choice. All this was about to start as I came on the school board. I liked the idea very much.

I was well received by the other members of the school board. The quickest bond I made was with the board chair, David Preus. We became very good friends. David came from a long line of Norwegian Lutheran ministers and was the senior pastor of University Lutheran Church of Hope. David is tall and outgoing and projects great strength. He is one of the nicest people I've ever met. He had a great career before him. A few years later, he became president of the American Lutheran Church.

Three of the seven school-board seats were up for election on June 10, 1969: David's, mine, and a third one. David said, "Harry, why don't you and I run together, as a team? Why don't we go out and get endorsements together? Maybe some of the endorsements that you can't get alone, I can get for you, and vice versa." I thought it was a great idea and generous on his part. He was sure to win the election easily. But I was new to city politics and my vote-getting ability was untested. David had in mind joint lawn signs, joint advertisements, joint appearances, and joint appeals for endorsements. That last part would be tricky because I was a DFLer and David was a Republican.

We went together to the Republican and DFL conventions to ask for their endorsements. The Republican convention was first in line. I was not sure how I would be received, but I found that I knew quite a few people there. A number of businesspeople I had met through the Urban Coalition were Republican delegates. David and I had our

The Reverend David Preus and I ran as a team when I made my first bid for the Minneapolis School Board in 1969. I had been appointed to the board earlier that year.

names placed in nomination for endorsement. No other names were submitted, and in a quick voice vote we were endorsed. It was a snap.

The DFL convention was a different matter. The idea of teaming with a Republican was more than some of those fierce DFLers could take. We fought through several ballots until finally I crossed the 60-percent mark needed for endorsement—but David did not. The delegates cast only one more ballot, and again, David's vote was short of 60 percent. We were disappointed, but we told the DFL delegates that we planned to continue to run together. We would simply say that I was DFL-endorsed and David was Republican-endorsed.

Our teamwork paid off on election day. David was the top vote-getter out of six candidates with 69,519 votes; I came in second with 63,475. That victory said a lot to the black community, which had only a smattering of success before in electing people of color. My supporters were also pleased after the election when my fellow board members chose me as the board's clerk, or number-two leader.

We soon faced a problem that had nothing to do with race. Relations between the district and its two teachers unions were worsening and heading for a breaking point. Salaries were the issue between teachers and the district. They were simply too low. In 1969–1970, teachers' salaries in the city ranged between $6,760 and $15,555 a year. I thought the teachers were underpaid.

They were people of such talent and were so deserving of a decent standard of living. I wanted to help them get higher salaries. But the school board felt it had little financial wiggle room. In those years, public education was funded primarily through local property taxes. Voters in Minneapolis were already up in arms about high property taxes. They would not stand for more.

A teachers strike began April 9, 1970. It would last fourteen days, long enough to make family life difficult for working parents throughout the city. We kept school doors open for two days after the strike began, hoping to give families extra time to find child-care arrangements. We couldn't afford to offer that service any longer, and we got no credit for doing that much. My home phone rang so often during the strike that I had to take it off the hook to get any sleep at night.

Many of our meetings during the strike occurred in the Minneapolis Public Schools administration building, which meant we had to cross the picket line every time we went inside. It was not something I did easily. My Teamster father had taught me to always respect a picket line. Besides, I was a labor-endorsed elected official. That meant something to me. So every time I entered that building, I felt I had to apologize to the picketers. "Look, we're getting close," I would say. "Don't feel insulted because we're walking across the picket line. We have to do that to settle the strike."

David Preus and I were "pro-teacher" board members.

We were eager to offer the unions enough compensation to satisfy them and end the strike. The wage and benefits deal that finally ended the strike was a stretch financially for the school district, so much so that it mustered only a four-to-three vote by the board.

The circumstances of that vote were a bit unusual. One morning during the strike, after an early meeting, I went to my office at the Urban Coalition. I had what I thought was a cold, but I could not think of taking a day off. I called my secretary into my office and began dictating a letter. Suddenly, I passed out. My secretary yelled for the other staff members to help revive me. I came to, but I had difficulty breathing. I went to the Mount Sinai Hospital emergency room, where I was diagnosed with pneumonia. My doctor decided to admit me to the hospital.

The next thing I remember is being in a room, surrounded by an oxygen tent. I was pretty sick. The phone rang. It was David Preus. He said, "Harry, we've got a pretty close agreement on our offer. . . . What are you doing in the hospital?" I told him I had pneumonia. He said, "What do you want me to do?" It occurred to me to ask him for a good Lutheran prayer. Instead, I said I would talk with my doctor about whether I could meet with my school-board colleagues. My doctor agreed to let me meet with two or three people at a time. So over the next few days, a steady parade to my bedside continued the negotiations, and that's where the final board vote took place. All the board members were in my hospital room as we agreed to a wage package that would boost average salaries by about $1,000 in the next year.

Tense as the teachers strike had been, it was only a prelude to the real excitement that soon hit the city's schools. It was time for the next step in desegregation. On November 24, 1970, we unveiled what we thought was a small start. It would "pair," or merge, almost all-white Hale School with racially mixed Field School, both elementary schools on the city's South Side. Kindergarten through third grade would attend Hale; grades four through six would be at Field. The neighborhoods surrounding the two schools were much alike aside from race. We thought starting with such similar schools so closely situated would be well received. Instead, the reaction was explosive. That November 24 meeting lasted five hours, as citizens who opposed the Hale-Field pairing angrily objected. Afterward, police followed both Superintendent Davis and me to our homes and guarded us through the night.

But we knew something that the desegregation opponents failed to grasp: a federal judge was soon going to insist that Minneapolis schools be integrated. Segregated schools violated the equal-protection clause of the U.S. Constitution and would not be allowed to stand. The NAACP filed a lawsuit that was being taken seriously by the federal courts. It was time to force the issue of race in Minneapolis schools, and only a lawsuit would make that happen. The school board knew it could not wait. We needed to get a citywide desegregation plan ready. We wanted it to be like the Southeast Alternative Program, offering students and their families a menu of choices to lure them to schools outside of their neighborhoods.

We knew it would be difficult. Where would we find all the teachers we would need? How would we put so many different approaches to teaching and learning within reach of every family in the city? How would we handle families who wanted all of their children in the same school? Superintendent Davis had answers. He proposed to divide the city into three zones—north, east, and west—

and put a superintendent in each zone. All the teaching styles would be offered somewhere within each zone. Each school would have a program designed to attract students who lived outside that school's traditional geographic boundaries.

We knew we had a big public education job ahead of us. What none of us fully understood was that we had a political challenge before us as well. If I had understood public opinion better at the start of 1971, I might not have decided to run for mayor.

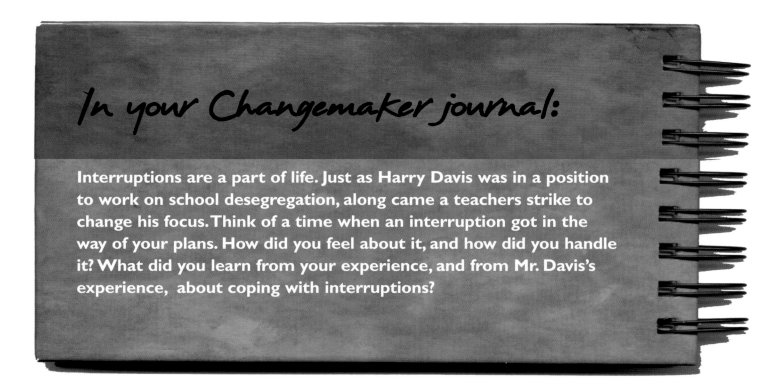

In your Changemaker journal:

Interruptions are a part of life. Just as Harry Davis was in a position to work on school desegregation, along came a teachers strike to change his focus. Think of a time when an interruption got in the way of your plans. How did you feel about it, and how did you handle it? What did you learn from your experience, and from Mr. Davis's experience, about coping with interruptions?

Campaigning

DFL endorsed

Harry Davis for Mayor

MY WORK WITH the War on Poverty, the Urban Coalition, the school board, and Golden Gloves gave me some definite ideas about city leadership. I knew the issues that were dividing people in Minneapolis, and thought I knew what it would take to bring them together. The various camps were not that far apart, it seemed to me. Most people wanted a decent life for everybody of all races. They were all talking about good education, affordable housing, high-wage jobs. I knew that people who were angry at another race often did not really understand the other side's position.

I thought it should be possible for Minneapolis people to get along and achieve the goals they shared, especially if they had a mayor who worked hard at bringing people together.

Unfortunately, the 1969 election had not given Minneapolis such a mayor. Art Naftalin had stepped down because of ill health. I could not help but be discouraged as the race to succeed him unfolded that year. The one DFLer was knocked out in the primary. The two candidates on the June ballot were Dan Cohen, the Republican president of the City Council, and Charlie Stenvig, a political independent and the president of the Minneapolis Police Federation. I did not think much of either of them. Neither had been an ally of Mayor Naftalin. Neither made equal opportunity for all races a top priority. The campaign turned on Stenvig's tough talk about law and order in the streets and lower property taxes. The city's working-class neighborhoods pushed Stenvig over the top.

For people who liked Naftalin's leadership, Mayor

Art and Fran Naftalin looked on as I filed my candidacy for mayor of Minneapolis in 1971. Fran filed that day for the Minneapolis Library Board, a position she won and held for many years.

right thing. The more liberal side, most evident in the black community, wanted immediate improvement in the lives of people of color. I was close to both camps, and I thought I could bring them together. Much of the political discussion in Minneapolis in those years boiled down to a question of how soon change could come. Many times I found myself in conversations like this: "Here are our goals. They're your goals and the other side's goals too. There may be a little different route that you'll want to take than the other side, but the result is the same. Now, how do you want to get that done? Do you want to get that done ten years from now, or in three or four years?" I worked to develop strategies for change that were both prompt and realistic, and could be supported by both sides. I began to think that I was in a unique position, and that it might be that I was there for a reason. That sense was at the root of my desire to run for mayor.

Stenvig was a disappointment. He had no new programs to propose, and he stood in the way of ideas that came from the City Council. He did not work well with businesses or racial minorities. Yet he was popular. Like another political figure a generation later, Governor Jesse Ventura, Mayor Stenvig was admired for his plain talk and independence. But unlike Governor Ventura, he was trying to keep things as they were, not make changes.

Of course, my business was change—positive change for the poor and minority communities of the city. I saw that the people pushing for change fell into two camps: conservative and liberal. Businesspeople were on the conservative side. They wanted change to come gradually and voluntarily, with nobody being forced to do the

The need to begin mixing black and white children in the same schools put Mayor Stenvig and me at odds. I was angry at him for opposing school desegregation. He said things like, "There isn't going to be any integration here." That was stupid. Once a federal judge issued an order, the school board would be in no position to resist, no matter what the mayor said. Mayor Stenvig wanted people to believe that those of us on the school board who favored desegregation wanted to force kids to take long bus rides to school and to spend so much in the process that property taxes would soar. It wasn't true. But when he made a claim, it was hard to refute.

Mayor Stenvig and his friends tried to create a third political party called the T Party, short for Taxpayers Party. The new party wanted to cut taxes, but it soon seemed more interested in blocking school integration than in changing tax policy. When the school board had open meetings, T Party people would pack the auditorium. One of those meetings, at the old Vocational High School, lasted twelve hours, from 5:00 p.m. until 5:00 a.m., even though we limited speakers to three minutes each. We heard the same speech, over and over again. Some speakers made a point of walking close to me and muttering foul language. At one point, a man sneaked along the side of the room and ran up on stage. As he got close to me, he spit. He missed me, and to his surprise, a plainclothes police officer came out from behind a curtain and hauled him away.

Mayor Stenvig himself seldom spoke about the school issue. He was not much of a public speaker. But his friends kept hammering away against school desegregation because they believed he would win reelection if he could play on people's fears. Fear was the biggest factor in city politics in 1971. To fearful white people, mixing black and white children at school meant black people moving next door, dating their children, exposing them to crime.

The business leaders I worked with on the Urban Coalition wanted to find someone they trusted to run against Mayor Stenvig in 1971. They encouraged me to go for it, and said they would give me a leave of absence from the Urban Coalition while I ran. They also contributed seed money for a campaign. With their support, I announced my candidacy for mayor on January 19, 1971. As I did, I couldn't help but notice that many of my supporters lived in the suburbs, not the city, and would not be voting in the June 8 city election.

The most important encouragement I received came from Charlotte. She was always in my corner. She was a busy mother and grandmother in those years. Evan

The family posed for a professional portrait, which I later used in my mayoral campaign literature. Charlotte is holding Evan; behind us are Ricky, Rita, and Butch.

turned three in 1971, and Ricky was in high school. Charlotte was used to managing the home front, and she was good at it, but for the children's sake, she would often say, "Harry, you've got to spend some time at home." One night, Evan was drowsing on her lap as they watched the local TV news. I was at one of our long school-board meetings. The news included a sound bite of me speaking. She roused Evan and said, "Look, there's your daddy. That's probably the only time you'll see him today."

My work was spilling into our home in some unpleasant ways. Even before I was a candidate for mayor, I was getting hateful anonymous phone calls at all hours. They were more annoying than frightening. But there were more of them when I became a candidate for mayor, and they were more threatening. I began to worry about my family's safety and asked for police protection. Starting several months before the election, I had squad cars around my house at all hours of the day and night. I had a bodyguard who followed me wherever I went. The police asked Ricky to ride in a squad car to school, even though we lived within walking distance of Central High. He hated the idea, but he did it. When Charlotte took Evan to Montessori school, a squad car followed her there and back. The fact that the police seemed to be taking the threats seriously made us nervous. They offered me a permit to carry a gun, but I said no. "There's no use in me carrying a gun if I don't know who is going to be shooting at me," I said. "I don't have an equal chance. I'd just be a dead

man with a gun in my hand or in my pocket. I can be dead without it." Then I added, "If you think I'm in such danger that I need a gun, you need to get me more protection."

Not long after that, an FBI agent, a black man, was assigned to guard us. The local police said they invited the federal agents to take over because I was receiving hate mail from out-of-state places like Racine and Eau Claire, Wisconsin. But I also suspected that the police lost interest in protecting me when I said in a campaign statement that I wanted to hire more black cops. It was right after I made that statement that I was given an FBI guard. He was very kind. He would say, "Don't worry, we're here. You may not see us, but we're here." We would look out our window every night and see one or more cars parked nearby with their parking lights on. We liked knowing those cars were there for us.

For a time, I got a mean phone call every morning before I went to work. My pattern was to drive east on Thirty-seventh Street and north on Chicago Avenue to downtown Minneapolis. At Thirty-sixth and Chicago stood a pizza place with a big billboard on its roof. The voice on the phone generally said something like, "Good morning, Nigger Mayor, which you're never going to be, because when you go by Thirty-sixth and Chicago today, we're going to shoot you through the head. We're going to kill you, and your wife is going to be a widow."

My FBI bodyguard was soothing. He said, "Mr. Davis, don't worry. We'll take care of that." The police and FBI who arranged to stake out the corner met with me and laid out a plan: "When he calls tomorrow, say to him, 'Now that you're going to kill me, let's see how brave you are. Yesterday, the police permitted me to get a gun, and I bought a .45 automatic. You've got a high-powered rifle. Let's see if you've got guts enough to stand from behind that billboard and face me.'" The FBI agent said, "Now, don't worry," as he gave me a bulletproof vest to wear. "If he is there, we'll get him before he raises his hand." I delivered the message as I was told. No bullets flew at Thirty-sixth and Chicago that morning or any other morning during the campaign.

But the calls continued for weeks thereafter. The tactic changed, with the callers threatening to blow up my house. In response, the FBI installed a security system and also brought two guard dogs to the house, a female German shepherd and a male half-German shepherd and half-husky. The female dog would stay inside the house and the male would sleep outside, even in the snow and cold. The idea was that if anyone approached the house from the outside, the male dog would warn the dog on the inside. She would in turn get our attention, so we could trigger the alarm and summon the police. The callers were quickly aware of the dogs' presence. "You've got two dogs," the voice said one morning. "You'll soon have two dead dogs. We're going to shoot those dogs." Other callers would say, "The police that are walking around your house are not your friends. The guard you've

Grandson Corey with guard dogs Shep and Brute, our watchdogs during my 1971 mayoral campaign.

got is not your friend." The most frightening call came the day Ricky was running in a regional track meet at Macalester College in St. Paul, representing Central High School. The caller said, "I understand Central High School won the city track meet and you're going over to Macalester to watch your kid run. That's a wide-open place there. What if we shoot Ricky as he wins the track meet? Don't you think it's time that you just give up?"

Miserable as the calls made all of us, they were particularly hard on Charlotte. At home all day, she took some of the worst of them. The dogs were her daily companions and a huge attraction for Evan and our grandson,

Ricky leads the way, easily winning the 220-yard dash at the regional high-school track meet in 1971 at Macalester College. He ran knowing that I had received an anonymous telephone call earlier that day threatening his life.

Corey. Fortunately, the dogs loved kids. Those little boys could do anything to them and the dogs would never growl or snap back. Still, the boys were only two and three years old, and the dogs were large. They could mow the boys down. One day, when the boys were in the backyard with the dogs, Evan suddenly ran in to the house, calling, "Mama, Mama, where's the paper?" Charlotte said, "It's right over there. What do you want the newspaper for?" Evan said, "Shep's got Corey down and I've got to whip her with the paper!" Shep, the female dog, had knocked Corey flat and was still playfully licking him as Charlotte raced outside.

People often asked me during the campaign what it was like to be the first black person to be a major-party candidate for mayor. I always answered in positive terms. I'd say that running for city office seemed an impossible dream when I was a child, and how good it was that such a thing was now possible. I could also have mentioned that there a bodyguard was at my side and the reason he was there, but I never did.

I won DFL endorsement fairly easily, and I thought that meant that the backing of labor unions would be a sure thing. In city elections, DFL endorsement and labor endorsement usually go hand in hand, but that was not the case for me. Even before the party's convention, the city's Teamsters Union—my dad's union—endorsed Mayor Stenvig. That hurt. Less than a week after the convention, the city's Central Labor Union Council also went with Mayor Stenvig. The building trades were cool to minority membership, and that had something to do with the union's choice. The *Minneapolis Star* quoted an anonymous labor leader saying as much: "Let's face it. The color thing had a lot to do with it."

The loss of labor support was a major blow to my campaign. Still, I pressed forward. I set out to make the most of the few advantages I did have. I knew that the black community was behind my candidacy, but I also knew that too many black people were not registered to vote. So a big voter-registration push was launched by some of the organizations that knew me well—the NAACP, the Urban League, and Phyllis Wheatley and Sabathani Community Centers. I headed the boards of directors of both Phyllis Wheatley and Sabathani in those years. Scores of people helped with our registration campaign. I like to think that my campaign made voters out of nonvoters for many elections to come.

I was popular among young people, and that inspired my campaign committee to recruit college students as volunteers. I went to college campuses in Minneapolis and St. Paul to speak to classes and ask for help. My pitch seemed to be particularly effective at Macalester. Students from that St. Paul college started showing up regularly at my campaign headquarters in the old Produce Bank Building in downtown Minneapolis. They would distribute literature, stuff envelopes, make phone calls, and do whatever else needed doing. We had little stickers reading "I'm

Campaigning takes many forms. I helped serve a meal at a community meeting in April 1971.

Seeking the youth vote, May 1971.

just wild about Harry" that they plastered all over town.

I was still Upper Midwest director of the Golden Gloves boxing program and had just completed a term as the organization's national president. My boxers, past and present, were in my corner. They put on a couple of boxing shows to benefit my campaign.

I accepted every possible invitation to appear at candidate forums and meetings. Sometimes I wound up debating an empty chair. Mayor Stenvig and I had five joint appearances over a five-month campaign, but only two of them were debates. The first was a fairly tame exchange. The second debate was livelier. More than 250 people showed up. The mayor came in carrying a large three-ring notebook. His supporters were there in force, and when the audience could ask questions, all they wanted to talk about was school busing for the sake of racial integration.

The key question was, "What would you do if the federal courts ordered the Minneapolis school system to bus children for school desegregation?" Mayor Stenvig boasted, "I would override the court's order." It was a ridiculous answer, but the crowd loved it. When I was asked for my response, I said, "You must understand that the Minneapolis school district is a part of government. Our federal government has preemptive authority over the fifty states. The United States Supreme Court has ordered the federal courts to make sure that schools around the country be racially balanced. If it takes busing to get racial balance, that has to be done. We have the option: we

either desegregate our school system or the court will. We would rather not wait to be directed. My concern is the children of the city of Minneapolis. I would say this: If *you* had been discriminated against and the federal government says that it's time to end that, if the shoe were on the other foot, you wouldn't be making these statements. The mayor of Minneapolis must understand that he's the mayor of all the people, all the children, regardless of the color of their skin. He has to carry out a federal court order. If I'm elected mayor, that's what I will do."

There were a few hisses in response and only a smattering of applause. The room was warm and the crowd was restless. It suddenly occurred to me that this debate could have an ugly ending and that I ought to say something to calm things down. So at my next opportunity to speak, I said, "I hope that we don't allow this campaign to get into a confrontation. Whoever you elect as the mayor is going to be the mayor of all of us, whether we like it or not. This debate is not intended to be a contest of power or strength. It's just a chance for you to hear each of us answer the questions you have, and for you to see which person you want to be mayor." On my way out of the room that night, a couple of Stenvig supporters spit at me.

I did a lot of speaking in that campaign. My leave of absence from the Urban Coalition gave me time to meet with a lot of groups and to campaign door-to-door too. I enjoyed door-knocking. It was especially fun in my old North Side neighborhood. People were so happy to see me. Fathers and mothers would call their children to the doors. "This is the man on the school board who is running for mayor," they would say. They wanted their children to know that someone whose color matched theirs could do such a thing.

My campaign committee urged me to spend more time in northeast Minneapolis. We were running way behind there, in an area that DFLers could usually count on for support. I had doors slammed in my face, many times. After a few days of that treatment, I got a call from one of the city's prominent DFLers, Bob Short. The big Irishman owned several hotels, including the Leamington and the Nicollet. Bob said, "I'd like to have you come down to the Nicollet Hotel. I'm going to have some people there to talk to you." I appeared as requested, and found Senator Hubert Humphrey waiting for me. He said, "Harry, I heard that you've had some problems in northeast Minneapolis. Don't let that upset you. You're going to find some people in Northeast who are going to really get behind you."

Later that day, I was back on the streets of northeast Minneapolis. I had stopped at only a few houses when a car pulled up alongside me. Out of it jumped Hubert Humphrey and the city's DFL congressman, Don Fraser. They said, "Harry, we're coming to give you some help." They offered to go with me and introduce me as their choice for mayor. They spent the rest of that afternoon with me and the next day too. Then Hubert had to go back to Washington, but Don stayed with me several

Senator Hubert Humphrey was very supportive of my mayoral campaign.

Governor Wendell Anderson also gave me strong, visible support.

more days. It may have been the nicest gesture I ever witnessed in political life.

The April 27 primary foretold what was to come in the June 8 election. It narrowed the field of seven candidates to two, Mayor Stenvig and me. But the numbers weren't close. He got more than forty-nine thousand votes; my total was just under twenty thousand. I knew that my general-election prospects were not good.

A few weeks later, a *Minneapolis Star* Metro Poll predicted I would lose by a devastating three-to-one margin. The same poll found that, despite all the talk about the schools, the issue most important to voters was the same one that Mayor Stenvig rode on into office in the first place: law and order. People had been led to believe by his campaign that only he, as a former police officer, could provide adequate public safety. In response, I stepped up my attacks on his leadership of the police department as mayor. The illegal drug trade in Minneapolis was out of control, I charged. Moreover, I said, the mayor was lax in responding to complaints about police brutality.

In so many ways, it was a wonderful campaign. We did so many things right and rallied so many fine people to our side. We struck down a racial barrier and helped ease people's fear about school integration. We brought white and black people together in a way that no previous citywide campaign had. I felt like a fighter, in good shape and pumped up for the next round, when the family gathered in their Sunday-best clothes at the Nicollet

Hotel on election night. We had dinner there before the usual election-night party. In addition to Charlotte and the children, my brother, Menzy, and sister Dooney were there. There were also two empty seats at the table. That was Charlotte's surprise. Just as I began to wonder who was missing, in walked Ray and Mae Hatcher. My old Phyllis Wheatley coach and mentor had come all the way from Detroit with his wife to be with me that night. The mood was festive. "Harry Davis for Mayor" signs were everywhere. I had both a victory speech and a concession speech written and in my pocket. It was hard to believe that this was the end.

But the evidence was in hand soon enough. Mayor Stenvig was reelected with more than 70 percent of the vote. He carried every one of the city's thirteen wards. The polls had been closed for less than two hours when I decided it was time to pull the concession speech out of my pocket. In front of me, sitting on the floor in a semicircle, were perhaps one hundred of the students who had been volunteers in my campaign. I know that a good speaker looks right at his audience, but I could not look for long at those dejected students. I was aware that some of the girls were crying. After I was through speaking and the TV lights were off, one tearstained girl said to me, "Oh, Mr. Davis, I so wish that you could have been mayor. You would have been a great mayor." I replied, "One of the things that you have to remember is that you never know unless you try. When you try, you've got to be able to accept the disappointment of losing. Who knows? This may be the part of your life that sets the stage for you. Who knows? Someday you may be mayor."

That girl's name was Sharon Sayles. Twenty-two years later, as Sharon Sayles Belton, she was elected mayor of Minneapolis—the first African American mayor in the city's history. During her 1993 election-night victory speech, she called me to the podium and told her supporters about our exchange on June 8, 1971.

For a while afterward, I felt that Minneapolis showed its true colors in the 1971 mayoral election—and those colors were ugly. But in time I came to understand that my campaign caught the crest of a wave of fear that would wash away quickly. I tried to say in the campaign that Minnesotans had no reason to be afraid. We are intelligent enough to understand that the Constitution means equal protection for every American citizen, not just citizens of one color. We are creative enough to find a way to extend equal opportunity to all, without being unfair to the majority. That message did not get through in time for me to be elected mayor. But that message was soon widely accepted. It is still the right one today.

My concession speech at the Nicollet Hotel, June 8, 1971. From left: Ray and Mae Hatcher, Yvette and Butch Davis, me and Charlotte.

In your Changemaker journal:

Changemakers like Harry Davis often try something new, knowing that they might not succeed. Describe a time when you tried something new. How did it go? Did you try more than once? What did you learn about trying new things? Are you more or less willing to try something new in the future?

A project for your class:

Who are some of the changemakers in your city today? Make a list of three or four of them, then compose letters to send to them, asking them to describe a change each is trying to make. Ask them what tactics they are using, what obstacles they are encountering, what personal skills they are employing to succeed. Ask them what alternatives they are considering if their tactics fail. Ask an adult to find their addresses and help you mail your letters to them. See what response the return mail brings!

Fulfilling 16

MY RACE FOR MAYOR did not end my involvement in my city or my quest for equal opportunity, not by a long shot. I was still the executive director of the Urban Coalition and still a member of the Minneapolis School Board. I had plenty of work to do on both.

When I returned to the coalition, it picked up on an issue I had discussed in my campaign: improving relations between the police and the people they protected. The coalition board liked what I had said about that subject and wanted to act. Soon there was a call throughout the city for block parties to be attended by cops on the beat so residents could meet their protectors in a friendly setting, rather than a hostile one. The annual block parties we started then continue every summer to this day in much of the city.

Minneapolis schools still had too many black children clustered in too few schools, and too many white children in all-white schools. At the school board, we were moving to change that. On April 25, 1972, we voted five-to-two to begin a citywide desegregation plan, affecting forty-two of the city's one hundred public schools. It was a five-year plan—too slow to suit me, and I said as much. Still, it was a risky move, given the opposition to desegregation that was evident during my campaign for mayor just a year before. But to my surprise, on the night of our historic vote, about half of the four hundred spectators in the meeting room burst into applause when our votes were counted. My friend David Preus spoke eloquently about why we were acting: "Justice in the public schools means equal educational opportunity for all children. As long as we require children in money-poor families to cluster together in central-city schools, isolated from the majority of privileged children, we cannot provide them equal educational opportunity."

The school board acted just a few weeks before Judge Earl Larson found Minneapolis guilty of wrongly keeping white and black children separated in public schools. He ordered us to make the very changes we had just voted to approve. That order meant there would be no going back. School desegregation was on its way in Minneapolis. Not even Mayor Charlie Stenvig could stop it, and voters quickly saw how wrong he had been.

In the 1973 election Mayor Stenvig was defeated, but not by me. I had a new job: special assistant to the publisher of the *Minneapolis Star* and *Tribune.* I became one of the first black executives at a major Minneapolis corporation.

My assignment was an interesting one. I was to help the newspapers' publisher, John Cowles Jr., bring a new professional sports stadium to downtown Minnneapolis, preferably on land in the Elliot Park neighborhood near the Star and Tribune building, on the east side of downtown. That part of Elliot Park was a slum. I would work on finding new and better homes for the people who lived where the Metrodome would be built, and on improving the quality of the housing that would remain. It meant continuing to try to make things better for low-income people, just as I had done at the coalition. I would also keep working with Minneapolis business leaders as the Star and Tribune's representative to the Chamber of Commerce and the Downtown Council. I felt right at home.

The Star and Tribune gave me as much time as I needed for my school-board duties, my work with organizations like Phyllis Wheatley and Sabathani Community Centers, and boxing. Boxing is what brought me to the party—that is, to recognition and opportunity in Minneapolis. I never forgot that. I stayed involved in box-

ing, one way or another, for more than fifty years.

I had moved from coaching to administration of the Golden Gloves boxing program in 1960. I was in charge of the program for the entire Upper Midwest region, including North Dakota, South Dakota, and Minnesota. Our organization sponsored a major tournament in Minneapolis every year, in addition to special shows and summer camps. We established the rules for all our member clubs, including ones at each of the eleven settlement houses in Minneapolis.

In 1969, I was elected president of the Golden Gloves Association of America. That put me in a good position to bring the national tournament to Minneapolis, which I did, in 1972. It brought boxers from thirty-one cities to Minneapolis for six days of competition. Thousands of volunteers, including many of my former boxers, helped stage the event. It was a high point in boxing history in our region.

At about that same time, I was named a member of the U.S. Olympic Boxing Committee. Later, I also joined the World Olympic Boxing Committee. That meant a lot of travel for me, to places like Las Vegas, London, and Madrid. I traveled both for meetings and as one of several managers for the U.S. boxing teams. The most fateful of those trips was one I didn't make. In 1980, I was supposed to accompany the U.S. Olympic boxing team to Warsaw, Poland. Because our plane was delayed in Minneapolis, Charlotte and I and two Minnesota boxers missed the flight from New York to Poland. The flight that we missed crashed on the runway in Warsaw. All eighty-seven people aboard were killed. We were stunned to realize that had we been on that plane, our lives would have been lost too. It was a horrible tragedy, and a sad setback for amateur boxing in the United States.

My favorite Olympic memories involve the summer games in Los Angeles in 1984. The United States had its best boxing team yet. It included one boxer who would go on to be the heavyweight champion of the world, Evander Holyfield. Of our twelve first-team fighters, nine won gold medals, one won a silver, and one won a bronze. It was an amazing sweep.

I was team manager, which put me in charge of the team's housing, meals, transportation, credentials, and other logistics. We were assigned to a large complex at the University of Southern California that included track and field, polo, swimming and diving, and boxing. We competed on the campus where we were housed. Each meal was served outdoors in big tents and offered an amazing array of fresh fruits and vegetables, meats and fish, and an abundance of milk to accommodate the various dietary needs of the athletes. Each of our boxers had a daily diet to follow. The coaches ate with them to make sure they ate what they should. It was always a little bit of a thrill to walk into a tent at mealtime and see athletes from various countries wearing the warm-up clothes of their teams, gathering and talking in a babble of languages. A swimmer from Germany might be next to a track star from South Africa and a boxer from Minnesota. Whether they spoke the same language or not, they understood each other and got along well.

I was housed in the Olympic Village with our boxers. We were in apartments that had four bedrooms clustered around a living room, a kitchen, and a little dining room. I assigned two fighters to each bedroom. Our first and second teams, twelve boxers each, were housed in the same building but in separate clusters. Also with the team were four coaches, two doctors, two nurses, and judges and referees—about three dozen people in all. I assigned three first-team boxers and three second-team boxers to each of the four coaches and made them responsible for seeing the athletes through their schedules, monitoring their diets and training, and keeping track of their uniform and equipment requirements.

The crucial thing for Olympic boxers is to get through the weigh-in. A boxer who does not weigh what he should for his division is disqualified. The coaches and doctors worked together to get the boxers past that hurdle. Boxers who come in overweight have an hour in which to shrink down. It's possible to lose four or five pounds in an hour, but the effort required leaves a body weak for a day or so afterward. Competitors watch for that, and try to take advantage of boxers who had to bring their weights down quickly to qualify at weigh-in. I was often involved in conversations with coaches and boxers about helping boxers get through the weigh-in with ease. I also helped scout other countries' teams and shared my observations about their strengths and weaknesses.

Charlotte did not come with me to Los Angeles. She was active in the Links, a national organization for black women, and was attending their convention in Philadelphia while I was in Los Angeles. That meant that sixteen-year-old Evan was home alone—or would have been, if I had not arranged for him to join me in L.A. It happened that we had an extra bed in the second-team suite because one boxer went home early. I got Evan all the credentials necessary to put him in that bed. His roommate? Mike Tyson, the future heavyweight champion and boxing's bad boy of the 1990s. At the time, Mike seemed like a fine choice to bunk with Evan. Mike was only seventeen then, the youngest member of our team, and still much under the sway of his manager. He was a much tamer person in those years than he became a few years later after his manager died. Evan had the time of his life. He ate with the team; he traveled in official Olympic Village minivans with the team; he wore an official warm-up suit along with the rest of the team. He told me afterward that he even signed autographs when asked, just like the other boxers did.

The U.S. boxing team that year was exceptional, not only in boxing skill but in character. It was a group of fine young men. Our relationship was such that if the boxers needed anything, either equipment or something of a per-sonal nature, they called me. They were bright kids. They were not overly boastful, but they had plenty of self-confidence. Of course, they were kids, and kids need guidance. The adults who lived with the team often discussed how best to give each athlete the guidance he needed. Still, after living with the team for nearly a full month, I came away believing anew in the power of boxing to shape boys into admirable young men.

Holyfield, the future heavyweight champion, was very easy to work with. He was dedicated, confident, always in good shape, and pleasant to everybody. He was cheated out of a gold medal in Los Angeles. In his semifinal bout, the crowd was so noisy that no one could hear the bell ring. Holyfield hit his opponent and knocked him unconscious after the bell had rung. The judges debated what to do for some time before disqualifying Evander from that match. Their decision caused a howl of protest. Evander ended up with the bronze medal in the light-heavyweight division. His reaction to what happened made us proud. He did not fuss and fume that he had been cheated; he thanked his opponent, shook hands with the referees, and bowed to the judges. He handled himself with a lot of grace.

For every athlete, the Olympic games offer a powerful lesson. Young athletes work and sacrifice for years to get there, only to find that their competitors have done the same thing and are just as deserving. Athletes develop a great deal of respect for each other. They live with athletes from other countries and develop friendships that cross barriers of language and culture. Rarely does bad sportsmanship mar an Olympic event. Competition is keen at the Olympics, but so is the recognition that other athletes just might be the better performers. Athletes come away thankful for the experience, even if they don't win. I'm thankful for the experience too. The 1984 Olympic Games topped off my lifelong love affair with amateur boxing.

I often told my boxers, and anyone else who would listen, that the boxing ring, the squared circle we enter as boxers, is an imitation of life itself. "There's the squared circle," I would say. "That's where you are headed. That's life. You are in training to go into that circle and be something in life. If you want to succeed there, you must prepare your body, your mind, and your spirit. If you prepare today as boxers to enter this squared circle, then when you are an adult and must perform in life's larger circle, you will know what to do." That's what boxing did for me. It's what I hope I taught every young boxer I've known.

These were the trophies the U.S. boxing team I headed won at the 1976 Britain-USA team match in London.

In your Changemaker journal:

Review the things you are doing to prepare your body, mind, and spirit for adult life. If you could add one thing to your training, what would it be? Share your idea with a parent or an adult you trust.

Harvesting 17

I ASSOCIATE 1984 with something other than the Los Angeles Olympics. It is the year in which I battled cancer.

In 1983, during a routine physical exam, a bump was discovered in my groin, where the leg and abdomen connect. My doctors ordered a biopsy, a surgical procedure in which a small amount of tissue is removed and analyzed for disease. The tissue was analyzed by an oncologist, or cancer specialist, whom I came to know well: Dr. I. E. Fortuny. He determined that I had cancer, and that it was already present in my lymph glands as well as in the tumor in my groin. He wasted no time. The tumor and other tissue were immediately removed, and my belly was cut open so the doctors could check my liver. Knowing whether my liver was diseased would help my doctors decide what more they needed to do to defeat the cancer.

Charlotte and all four of my children were at the hospital as I had surgery, waiting for news. The report was serious, but not catastrophic: I had Hodgkin's disease, or lymphatic cancer. It appeared concentrated in the lymph glands of the groin. My liver did not appear to be affected. The doctors explained treatment options briefly to the family and later, in more detail, to me. We decided on chemotherapy, the first and second Mondays of every month, for a whole year.

It was a dreary prospect, but one I had to face. Most of the time, I went for treatments at Dr. Fortuny's office in south Minneapolis, near Abbott Northwestern Hospital. I was told not to drive home, so I would pick up Charlotte beforehand and she would sit with me during the long treatment sessions and drive me home afterward. I would be ushered to a reclining chair, like the ones used at blood banks, and a long needle would be injected into the blood vessels of my hands. That is, we started with my hands. After a few treatments, those vessels began to collapse, and the chemotherapist had to search for other vessels in my arms. During the last few sessions, she had to use hot towels to heat my arms in order to find blood vessels to use. Dr. Fortuny worked with a chemotherapist named Diana, a gentle, caring woman whose touches seemed to have healing power. I would arrive at noon. The first step was the injection of saline solution, both to avoid burning the skin with the strong poisons used in chemotherapy and to make sure the needle had been properly placed. By 12:30, the real stuff would begin flowing. It would not end until nearly 4:00 p.m., four long hours after my arrival. I would go home, knowing what would come next: extreme nausea. It was like a terrible case of stomach flu. I didn't stay sick very long, however. I often went to work the next day, though not at full strength.

That went on for a full year, twenty-four treatments in all. In between I had two bone-marrow biopsies taken from my pelvis bone. My doctors were also concerned about the cancer spreading. As the year of treatments drew to a close, Dr. Fortuny suggested that we do exploratory surgery to check my other organs. When I mentioned that to the family, they didn't like the idea. They felt I had endured enough surgery. My son Ricky had played football in school with a son of Dr. John Najarian, the famous chief of surgery at the University of Minnesota. Unbeknownst to me, Ricky contacted Dr. Najarian about my case. He in turn called Dr. Fortuny, and they arranged for me to check into University of Minnesota Hospitals (now Fairview-University Medical Center) for two days and be thoroughly examined by an oncologist there, Dr. B. J. Kennedy.

By coincidence, the year of my chemotherapy was also the first year of our involvement with a program called Christian Ashram. The Ashram originated in India as a Hindu spiritual discipline. Originally, it involved withdrawing from the world and praying in complete silence for several days. When it was adapted for western Christians, the requirement of intensive silence was dropped. But it was still a program of regular retreats, three or four days long, taking participants away from work and home to concentrate on God. Participants study the Bible, discuss lessons in small groups, and pray. One or more clergy leaders guide the sessions.

I had arranged for the new senior pastor at Hennepin Church, the Reverend David Tyler Scoates, to serve as our leader at the Ashram in 1984. It ran Thursday through Sunday, but Charlotte and I decided we needed to leave after the Saturday-evening session. I was to check into University of Minnesota Hospitals on Sunday for my two days of tests. On Saturday evening, before we left, Pastor Scoates led a healing service. Charlotte and I sat in the center of a circle as Pastor Scoates and other friends joined us and put their hands on us. Other participants then put their hands on them and so on until the whole group was connected by touch. I had a strange sensation as they prayed for me. It felt as if I were a light bulb and somebody had turned me on. I had the sensation of being very bright, like I was glowing. I was warm but not feverish, and everything I looked at seemed unusually clear and bright. When the prayer ended and hands were removed, the glow faded. When I described the sensation to Charlotte, she said she had felt the same thing while we were holding hands in the circle. We knew we had experienced something powerful.

The next night, I was admitted to University Hospitals and went through all the examinations in the book (and a few that weren't) over the next two days. My team of doctors met with me after all the results were in. "We cannot find a trace of cancer," they reported. Further surgery was not needed. The cancer was gone, and it has never come back.

When I describe my Ashram experience to people, they ask whether I believe I was healed at that prayer service. I know it played a role, but I believe that the knowledge and skill of the doctors and nurses also healed me. God works through medicine as well as prayer. God works through the love of family and friends. I was healed by the way Charlotte cared for me. She was my closest nurse and friend. I never saw her crying or giving up. She would go with me to the treatments and the checkups, and always be there for me when I came out. Her devotion said to me, "You can't give up. You've got to fight it." When I say today about my cancer, "The Lord was there and brought me through it," I think of all of those things. And I am grateful.

My faith in God has grown and become dearer to me as I have gotten older. I have seen the way God has touched people's lives and been with them through good times and bad. I see God more clearly in my own life as I reflect on my childhood and youth. It almost seems like a special power kept me from winding up in prison or addicted to drugs and on the streets. I have watched children and grandchildren grow and have seen them change as they have made a spiritual connection. I have come to a deeper understanding that God reveals himself through relationships with other people. More than ever, I see that it matters how we treat each other. It is a statement of faith to say of someone else, "That's my brother. That's my sister. Whatever happens to him or her happens to me. I will laugh when they laugh and mourn when they mourn. If they have nothing and I have something, I will share my something with them." To live a life of faith is to always strive to serve others.

So many people think that life slips away from you as you age. I believe just the opposite: you gain life as you get older. You first gain knowledge, the stuff of school and church and family. Then comes experience. As you put the two together, wisdom results. You learn that life is more than what you know or what you do. Its richness lies in the meaning you grasp and the viewpoint you develop along the way. For me, a key to grasping life's meaning has been faith in God.

After my recovery from cancer, I wanted to dedicate myself more fully to serving people. But I was aware that I had to set a slower pace. During my year of chemotherapy, I had several serious conversations with my doctors about my workload. Hard work may not cause disease, but hard work and stress make it more difficult for one's body to fight disease. I came to understand that it was important to my survival to reduce the stress in my life. I began to approach life differently. I tried not to let myself get so wrapped up in the routine conflicts that arose on the school board, the boxing federation, or at the office. When someone approached me in anger or opposition, I could almost hear an inner voice say, "Just let it go. Don't let it affect you."

I retired from the Star Tribune Company in January 1987 and from the school board after the 1989 city election. I had the satisfaction of knowing that I had helped mix the races in Minneapolis schools while keeping the quality of education high. I helped put people of color in the ranks of teachers and school administrators, and even helped hire one of my former Phyllis Wheatley athletes, Richard Green, as superintendent of schools. He was the first black superintendent in our district. To my great sorrow, Richard left Minneapolis to take the top school job in New York City in 1988—and he died fourteen months later during

an asthma attack.

I've stayed busy in the years since, keeping in touch with Phyllis Wheatley and Sabathani, staying active in several community boards and at Hennepin Church, and giving speeches every fall for the Greater Minneapolis United Way.

Minneapolis school superintendent Richard Green.

I spoke at Richard Green's installation as chancellor of the New York City school system. At right is New York governor Mario Cuomo.

Charlotte and I attend the Rotary Club Christmas party at the Minikahda Club, December 2001. We celebrated our sixtieth wedding anniversary in 2002.

The greatest blessing of my retirement years, of course, has been extra time for Charlotte and our growing family. Our four children have thus far given us thirteen grandchildren, enough to fill our hearts—and our house at our monthly family meetings—to overflowing. They represent a variety of racial colors and backgrounds, continuing the rich mixing of humanity that has always been characteristic of the Davis family.

Of the original Davis family of six children, only my sister Geraldine and I remain today. I started life as the baby of the family and wound up as the patriarch, the grandfather. I understand that role in a way that I believe is consistent with my Sioux Indian heritage. When Indians pray, they call God "Grandfather." I am the grandfather, which means I am to be the spiritual leader of my family. I am to be the guardian, watching out for the best interests of each one and for the continuity of the clan. When the Davis family gathers, which we do one Sunday each month, I always convene the group and offer the prayer. I ask the family members to join hands in a circle. I stand in the middle and speak. My grandchildren always seem eager for that moment—and I don't think that's only because they get to eat afterward. I think that those monthly prayers give even the youngest child a sense of belonging and a connection to something holy.

I have lived all my days in Minneapolis. Yet the place I knew as home is gone. The city's near North Side, the old Hellhole, is like a blackboard that was written on first by Jews, then blacks, then erased, rewritten, and erased once more. As I write these words, a large portion of the neighborhood is being swept away and rebuilt again. A massive new housing program is in the works, recently given the name Heritage Park. My hope is that it will bring new life to a neighborhood that I believe has a lot more to contribute to a great city.

Racial discrimination has not been eliminated in Minneapolis or anywhere else in the United States. But even in the old days, when racial hatred was often right out in the open, I felt lucky to live in Minneapolis. I always went to integrated schools. Both races always used city buses and streetcars freely. Our parks, pools, and lakes welcomed all comers. Our political leaders by and large have been people of goodwill who opposed racism.

That legacy ought to be both a point of pride and a summons to greater progress for today's generation. Minneapolis ought to be able to approach the whole question of diversity, of making the most of all of its human resources, with a leg up on other major cities. We have a lot less to overcome than most places.

It's time for a second wave of the civil-rights movement that had its first wave in the 1960s. A new push is in order for truly equal opportunity for all races—not just black and white, but Latino and Asian and Native American as well. For that to happen, there needs to be a coming together of people of color. In the middle of the twentieth century, the black community took the lead in combating discrimination. What's needed now is a coalition among many races. We need a way to bring the Asian American, Hispanic, Middle Eastern, and black communities together with white people of goodwill around an agenda of mutual advancement and support. We need to build the understanding that no one racial group is strong enough alone to make a great difference, but that together we can change society.

Our grandchildren were present for Charlotte's seventy-fifth birthday in August 2001, all but little Jaliya, who would be born three months later. Front row (from left): Myles, Melik, and Angelina. Second row (from left): Mikayla, Rekia, and Juwan. Third row (from left): Chloe, Corey, Ramar, and Jaylyn. Fourth row (from left): Charlotte, Grandpa, Grandma, and Nasstasha.

Our granddaughter Jaliya.

Trustworthy leadership is crucial to the continued advancement of people of color. This I know: to succeed, a leader has to be able to earn and keep people's trust. Trust is earned over time. It comes from being considerate of others, working hard, and staying honest. It comes from standing up for what's right, even if it's not popular. It comes from refusing to quit or give up. It comes from doing one's homework—preparing the body, the mind, and the spirit to step alone into the squared circle of life and apply oneself fully to the task at hand.

I learned those things from Gertrude Brown and Ray Hatcher, Hubert Humphrey and Cecil Newman, Art Naftalin and David Preus, and Charlotte NaPue Davis. I hope I taught them in turn to Rita, Butch, Ricky, and Evan Davis, and the many other young people whose lives I touched through the years. They are my legacy.

In your Changemaker journal:

Describe someone other than your parents whom you trust. What is it about that person that makes you trust him or her? What has that person done to earn your trust? What have you learned from that person about how to be trustworthy?

A project for your class:

Go to startribune.com on-line and search for the latest news about Heritage Park, the new housing development in Harry Davis's old neighborhood.

Index